BASEBALL

THE FANS' GAME

by

GORDON S. (MICKEY) COCHRANE

Reprinted by the

SOCIETY FOR AMERICAN BASEBALL RESEARCH

1992

INTRODUCTION

This book—out of print for half a century—is wonderful for two reasons. First its tone is real—a true rarity among player-written tomes. Although it's not an autobiography, you'll get a real sense of the Mickey Cochrane personality here, and remarkably little piffle. Second, it's full of nuggets that any baseball fan will treasure. There are plenty of surprises. Have you ever heard of a "George Stallings pitcher"? Would you have expected someone like Cochrane to have championed one-handed catching? Can you imagine Connie Mack cursing a blue streak on the bench? Did you know a yellow baseball was approved for minor-league use during the '30s? There are wonderful anecdotes about the stars of the '20s and '30s, too—some just tossed off in passing. Did you know, for example, that Wilcey

INTRODUCTION

Moore's best pitch was a "funny sinker ball?" And there are the tips: on technique, on strategy, on attitude, on playing the percentages, often delivered with the serene confidence of a man who has seen his "Big Inning" American League ("if one run is going to beat you, you might as well concede the game before you leave the clubhouse") dominate the senior circuit, where "one run is apparently important." I love that "apparently." *Baseball: The Fans' Game* may no longer be the best baseball book ever, as John Kieran called it in 1939, but it remains the best of its era, and SABR is proud to make it available once more.

Mark Alvarez
Publications Director
Society for American Baseball Research

GORDON S. (MICKEY) COCHRANE

BASEBALL

THE FANS' GAME

by

GORDON S. (MICKEY) COCHRANE

DEDICATION

To the Fans whose unfailing support has done so much to make baseball the tremendously popular game it is, this book is affectionately and gratefully dedicated, with the wish that it may give them just one moment of pleasure in repayment for their loyalty and the many thrills they provided me.

MICKEY COCHRANE

ACKNOWLEDGMENTS

IN the compilation of data and pictures for this work, which I hope will make the game better understood and, perhaps, better played, I am deeply grateful to Sam André of *Pic Magazine,* to the Detroit *Times,* and to Henry Edwards of the American League Service Bureau, for permission to reproduce many of the illustrations. I am also indebted to Charles Moran for aid in editing the manuscript.

G. S. C.

CONTENTS

CONTENTS

ILLUSTRATIONS

xiii

ILLUSTRATIONS

FOREWORD

FRANKLY, this is the best book on baseball that I ever read. But that's a minor point because it is much more than a deeply instructive and highly entertaining volume on our national pastime. It's a success story modestly told. It's an honest autobiography—to date—of a man whose personality and career have been the object of wonder and admiration of millions of our citizens, young and old. It's a lesson to those of us who still may profit by the example set by a man of courage and determination. It will be an inspiration to young readers who, in these pages, will learn how a young fellow, by intelligence, industry and dogged persistence, fought his way to the top of his chosen profession.

There are many baseball fans who think that Mickey Cochrane was the greatest catcher that baseball ever knew. He was one of the brightest individual stars in the glittering galaxy that brought pennants to Connie Mack's town, Philadelphia. As player-manager of the Detroit Tigers, he carried his team to two pennants and one world championship. He could serve and he could command; he could follow and he could lead. But better than all that, to those who knew him best he was a champion off the diamond as well as on it. No finer sportsman ever wore an athletic uniform. No firmer friend ever took the hand of any companion. And with it all he carries a genial vibrant spirit that makes everybody just a little better and happier for having seen or known Mickey Cochrane. It's a fine book that he has written. But nothing else could have been expected from a great fellow.

JOHN KIERAN

PROLOGUE

A STUBBY-LEGGED little kid, unpopular with his elders, tags along after his brother's gang and wins the disapproval of all of them. But after a time the gang becomes accustomed—and resigned—to the black-haired youngster.

"I suppose we'll have to take the kid along," one of them says. And the kid goes along. A year or less of this sort of thing, and the youngster becomes known as The Kid.

He follows the bigger boys to baseball games, horns in on their more adult diamond adventures, and even tries, in season, to play a little football with the older boys.

The Kid is no different from any other smaller brother. Consumed with an ambition to be an athlete, he tries and tries again until

PROLOGUE

the desire has become the goal of his life. He wants to be a professional athlete. Through high school and college The Kid keeps swinging, and one day is confronted with the proposition that every athletically minded youngster faces in course of time.

He wants to be a ball player!

I

BECOMING A PROFESSIONAL

K ID COCHRANE was a fair sort of football player. His desire to be a professional athlete was motivated as much by a thirst for baseball as by the lure of security which a successful career offered.

I had experienced little trouble with football. But baseball was a sport of another order. I tried the outfield. I tried the infield. I even pitched a couple of games; and once I caught, against Tufts. It was not versatility which shifted me around the diamond. The managers and coaches were anxious to find a place where I would be less likely to get hurt—where I could remain with the least damage to the team until it came my turn to bat. For I was a pretty good hitter.

BASEBALL

After the first year—my junior—in which I had made the team at Boston University, I went to Saranac Lake, New York, to play ball. One of my team mates was Joe Russell. He thought I had a longshot chance of making the grade in the toughest sport in which to get ahead.

On Russell's recommendation, Jiggs Donahue called me to Dover in the Eastern Shore League of Delaware for a trial. I played under the name of Frank King—for I was still in college—and signed up with the team only when it was agreed that I should have my release at the close of the season.

I was fast and I could hit, but if I thought I was a catcher the local baseball scribe at Dover pulled me up short. All too often there appeared in his reports of games a line which went something like this: "King, the Dover catcher, missed his usual number of foul flies."

Then a few weeks after my arrival I overheard one of the owners of the club in debate with Jiggs.

"The only benefit that guy King is to the

club is that he fills out the batting order," said the owner. "If he's a catcher, I'm one."

"He may not be a catcher," replied Donahue, "but he's a hitter. And as a hitter he stays. He'll learn to catch if I have to beat it into him, and you will not be sorry you kept him."

"Then he's your headache," snapped the owner.

With that faith in my hitting and speed, I determined then and there to become something more than a ninth man in the field. The first problem was foul flies. Admittedly, a catcher who cannot master the knack of getting under foul flies easily and naturally is not going to amount to much as a receiver. The only way I had ever learned anything in any sport was to practise, so practise catching foul flies I did. I made up a pact with Frank Knight, a big pitcher from Brown University.

In payment for warming him up and helping him to develop a new curve, he agreed to hit foul fungoes to me. We went to the Dover Park a couple of hours every morning for weeks. He would hit the flies for an hour and then I'd warm him up.

"I ruined myself as a pitcher," says Knight, today, "but I made a catcher out of you!"

No doubt he did contribute to the transition from Kid Cochrane of Boston University to Mickey Cochrane, the Philadelphia Athletics receiver, but it was not all in one jump, as his statement would indicate. At least it wasn't as far as Connie Mack is concerned. But that's getting ahead of myself.

Mr. Mack came close to having no problem with a red-faced fresh rookie catcher at all, for along toward the end of the Eastern Shore League campaign a knotty problem presented itself to the owners of the Dover club. The St. Louis Cardinals had offered $1500 cash in hand for that awkward catcher with the fair bat named Frank King. The Dover club offered to split the price with me.

But while King was of a mind to accept the fifty-fifty split of the ransom, Gordon S. Cochrane had a different idea. I had played with Dover under the condition that I would be made a free agent at the end of the season, and I felt that I could make a better deal for myself. I still had faith in my ability to hit, and I knew I could run. The catching, if it must be catching, might come in time. But, actually, I was toying with the notion that I was a born outfielder.

Coming up to the Saturday before Labor Day the officials of the club were of no mind to dicker with G. S. Cochrane. Seven hundred and fifty dollars was seven hundred and fifty. But I refused to weaken.

Dover had to win two of the three remaining games to win the pennant. I felt that my bat, regardless of my passed balls and dropped flies, would mean considerable in those contests. So on Saturday I met the officers of the club and issued an ultimatum.

"Gentlemen," I said, as augustly as I dared, "I either get my release, signed, sealed and delivered here and now, or you get a new catcher for tomorrow's and Monday's games!"

I got the release!

And, incidentally, I didn't hurt the Dover club in winning the pennant.

Tom Turner then made a deal for me with the Portland Club in the Pacific Coast League, and I went out there as a catcher. It was Tom who looked over the Gordon S. Cochrane on the agreement—a document which amounted to one sentence and a postcript on hotel stationery.

"What'd they call you in college?" he asked.

"Kid."

"Won't do," he replied. "Tell you what. You're from Boston, aren't you?"

"No, I'm from Bridgewater, Massachusetts," I answered.

"You're from Boston, as far as Portland is concerned," he said, and then, completely disregarding geography and ancestry: "In fact, you're a Boston Irishman named Mickey Cochrane."

And as Mickey Cochrane I went to the Pacific Coast League.

The postscript to that agreement with Turner? A notation that G. S. Cochrane would get transportation for two both ways, to Portland from Boston and from Portland to Boston, just in case. I was still doubtful of those foul flies.

Even after that season in Portland, I was dubious about catching. I thought to myself after a year in which I hit .333 in a faster league, or six points better than with Dover, that I was going to make myself over into an outfielder for 1925 if I was not sold!

But Turner was too fast. He traded me to Connie Mack for $50,000 cash, ten per cent of which I was to get. I never got it. But I did learn how to catch under Mr. Mack.

That sounds easy—the advancement, the becoming a professional. But it wasn't; and it is now a still harder row to hoe. In baseball it is all very well when you get up to the big money in the major leagues, but even the Class AA minor leagues of this day and age operate under a policy that is something less than perfect for the athlete.

But the climb up through the various stages of baseball, the development of a player through the chain system of a big league club with farms, or the climb without a big league attachment is the only way a boy can master the technique of the game today.

There are rare exceptions, of course, in which young men come off a college campus and make the big leagues in one or two steps. But these are rare. The most common method is to fight your way up the ladder.

Just recently I was talking about this with Jimmie Foxx, a great player who made the climb from Class D baseball.

"College baseball today is not as good as Class D ball," said Foxx, "yet kids coming out of college want to jump right into the big show. They are not giving themselves or baseball a chance in trying to make that upward move in one leap. They wouldn't go into a steel company and expect to start at the top, yet they do expect to do just that in baseball."

There are many hardships in minor league ball. The player, accustomed to comforts at home or at college, or the poor boy unaccustomed to any comforts, will find the row a tough one in Class D ball. The jumps from town to town are often far apart. They are made now-adays in buses. Most of the games are played at night. The hours are irregular, the hardships manifold, the night air often chill and unfavorable for baseball. But regardless of these conditions it is up this ladder, rung by rung, from Class D on through C, B, A, and AA, and finally to the majors, surmounting terrible infields, outfields in which a player risks his life chasing a fly ball with abandon, poor transportation, bad meals, loss of sleep, fumbling playmates, disappointed big leaguers, inept minor leaguers—all these are part of the picture and all are experiences which a major leaguer ought to have today.

"The desire to succeed," says Foxx, "will see a kid through if he has the stuff. I made it because of this desire. And I readily admit that anything I have, or ever will have, I owe to baseball.

"I admit I was a poor farm boy who would never have left the plow except for baseball. And baseball gave me the chance to develop. It gave me the opportunity to meet and know people that I could not have met except for baseball.

"Many times during the years I played down in the minors I was disillusioned. It is hard to sit on a bench in the big leagues and watch others you think less capable get the chances. But it is all part of the development. And when I got the chance after years of development I had confidence in myself, and fighting courage enough to escape the minors and stay off the bench."

I, too, went through discouragement of this sort after that second season in professional baseball. I'd had a good year at Dover and I'd done all right in Portland. But I was still dubious of that catching. I had hit .333, better than I'd done in Dover. And I was determined to try the outfield. Before I could do it, Turner sold me to Mack.

Reporting to the Athletics at Fort Myers, Florida, in the spring of 1925, doubts of my catching ability remained fresh in my mind. And this doubt was unquestionably transferred to my actions. Mr. Mack took one look and said:

BECOMING A PROFESSIONAL

"Son, I think you'd better work out at third base for a few days."

But after a few days at third base, even he, essence of patience that he was, thought my chest would not stand up under the wear and tear of stopping ground balls with it; and he moved me back to second stringer catcher behind Cy Perkins. Mr. Mack was quite doubtful of my ability to make the grade that season, but Cy insisted that I had the makings of a catcher and took me under his wing. Again, just as Donahue had expressed faith in me, I was determined to master the job. The way it worked out, I took over his catching job; but we remained friends through the remainder of my life in baseball, co-workers much of the time.

Again it was hard work, patience, and willingness to practise which helped. I caught two hours of batting practice every day for the remainder of that spring trip, and the first thing I knew the tricks of receiving suddenly came to me in natural movements. Perhaps the movements were not perfect, but practice made them seem so; and they worked.

These movements we will try to break down later, but there was one which Perkins taught me and which I tried to teach every young catcher who came my way. Mastering it protected my fingers through twelve and a half major league races. That is to become, in effect, a one-handed catcher; to stop the pitched ball always with the gloved hand, holding your right hand with the finger tips folded against the heel of the hand and the thumb laid along the side of the hand. After a time it becomes natural not to open the unprotected hand until the ball is in the well padded glove. In that way Cy and I caught 2500 games for Mr. Mack without ever suffering a broken finger!

The A's arrived at Shibe Park for the opening game of the season of 1925. Boston was the rival, and Cy Perkins was behind the bat for the Mackmen. Came the eighth inning and the Red Sox had tied the score. In our turn at the bat the bases were loaded when it came Cy's turn to hit, and Connie commenced to look for a hitter. On the mound, working for the Sox, was

BECOMING A PROFESSIONAL

Rudy Kallio; and Rudy had been something of a "cousin" of mine on the Coast in 1924.

When Connie looked over the bench for a pinch hitter, I remarked:

"Give me a bat, I can hit that guy."

"All right, son," said Connie, "go up there if you think you can."

I went up and singled to left, driving in the winning run. Cy took off his catching equipment just as the man crossed the plate, the boys on the bench told me much later, and said, "There goes Perkins' job on that base hit." I caught 135 games that season.

That, briefly, is how I became a ball player. I started out at B. U. something of a football sensation and played four years of varsity ball. I couldn't make the baseball team until my junior year, and even in my senior year they couldn't decide whether I was an acrobat or a shortstop; and I had my doubts after two years in professional baseball. I knew one thing; I could hit, and I felt if I applied ordinary intelligence to the other requirements, they would come. Hitters are still the goal for which every ivory scout is looking.

So you want to be a ball player! Learn to be a hitter, and the rest will come if you try hard enough.

While there are compensations in baseball, there are also headaches—headaches galore. All rookies do not deliver as the cocky Cochrane did when he saw a "cousin" on the mound, and when I say that I do not mean to be boosting my own stock. What I mean is that rookies, fresh and impudent, are one of the headaches of baseball life—whether you are a manager or a player. I recall one fresh kid who horned in on a workout of the A's down in Fort Myers.

This training-camp crasher forcibly wrenched the bat from the hands of a few of the A's power hitters, among them a fair hitter named Al Simmons.

"That's no way to hit," this oracle would say, grab the bat and then and there give a demonstration of how he did it. He became a nuisance, and quickly.

On that old A's club there was always a cure

for such fellows, and I believe it was about that time that George William Haas, called Mule by his friends, joined the club. If somebody didn't beat Mule to it, he was usually the one who would handle the cure. It was he who suggested to this would-be champion batsman that he go down to help out that fellow batting in a pepper game near first base. That fellow happened to be Ty Cobb.

All this bird needed was a suggestion. Down he ran to Cobb, grabbed the bat out of his hand and made his little speech about not being the proper way to hit. That was toward the end of Cobb's career in baseball, so I guess he was mellowing—or at least we thought so. He allowed the crasher to retain the bat and listened attentively to everything the "wise guy" had to say.

When Cobb thought the lesson was over, he asked the boy if he knew anything about base stealing. And the kid offered to help him!

But Cobb said he was pretty busy right then —his manager was a slave driver. Would the fellow mind coming around to the hotel that night, just to show him in private a few of the tricks of base stealing? "Glad to oblige," said our fresh young hero!

That night the kid went through the rudiments of his awkward slide on the mezzanine of the hotel at Fort Myers while most of the ball club looked on and howled. It may be that the fresh young "wise guy," who felt he could teach the greatest base stealer of them all something, learned the identity of his pupil; or perhaps the "strawberries" he suffered on his hips from sliding along a tile floor into a brass cuspidor rendered him null and void. Whatever the reason, his spell of tutoring the major leaguers was over. He never bothered us again.

The prize of the crack-a-loos or training-camp screwballs, though, in my memory appeared at Lakeland where the Detroit Tigers were getting in shape. This bird we dubbed "Curveball Mayer." He came into camp wearing one of those mail-order four-button suits like the Arkansas Traveler, a high celluloid collar, a red tie, a vintage of '98 straw hat, and brown bulldog button shoes. He might have walked right out of the pages of a '98 Sears-Roebuck catalogue.

"I just came over from Hot Springs," he told me, "and I says to myself if that Cochrane is depending much on Marberry, that Cochrane is the fellow I want to see."

How did he figure that out?

"Well," he said, confidentially, "that fellow Marberry will get hurt out there. He can't pitch."

This was something new to me, so I let the bird carry on. Remember always, when you are a manager, that many great ball players never saw shoes until they reported to a major league club. You can't afford to let any one pass without taking a look at him. So I listened to this fellow.

"I've got the fastest ball since Walter Johnson," he told me. "And I'm developing a curve that'll make anything you've got look silly."

Well, maybe this would be the one! I told him to get into a suit. He did, and came striding out of the clubhouse with a gait he must have copied from Joe E. Brown's interpretation of Elmer the Great. Right up to the pitching mound he breezed and without a by your leave shoved Tommy Bridges out of the way.

"Lemme have that ball," he demanded. I was catching by that time and tossed the ball to him. I warned him to warm up a bit.

"That's for sissies," he yelled, "get ready for this one, or it'll take your glove off."

I got set and he wound up like a combination of Firpo Marberry and Earl Whitehill, untangling himself in time to allow the ball to get loose from his grasp and wave its way to the plate. It would not have broken a pane of glass at five paces.

Before I could run him off the lot, he begged off for the day, excusing his lack of speed by saying that perhaps he was tired after all. He'd just driven all the way from Hot Springs, Arkansas, to Lakeland, Florida, without a stop; and maybe it took more out of him than he had reckoned. Well, the guy was either the biggest liar who ever lived or—but there was always the chance that he wasn't. So I told him to come back the next day.

BECOMING A PROFESSIONAL

The next day was a repetition of the first, and by that time the players took to kidding him and having some fun. I joined in the levity, and it made for a snappy workout.

Before the workout our friend popped off with every pitch. His main theme was the manner in which he fanned all the sluggers in the "Prairie league," where he'd supposedly been operating the season before. He boasted that nobody had ever hit a home run off him, and not until the pressure was put on him did he admit that there were no fences in the prairies where he played. By this time Perkins was getting bored with the conversation and thought he'd squelch this bird.

"Why, you can't pitch," said Cy; "even I can hit you."

"Oh, yeah," snapped back Curveball; "I only pitch to good hitters."

That chased Cy into the outfield.

As we were leaving the park to go back to the hotel, one of the men walking out with me noticed a big shiny La Salle car parked at the curb, just to the rear of his own—a light car type. Curveball was standing near by, and one of the fellows invited him to ride into town with us.

"No, thanks," said Curveball; "but if you like, I'll give you a lift."

"Is that yours?" I asked, pointing to this shiny job.

"Sure," said Curveball, smiling. Then, looking right at Cy Perkins with a grin, he said, "Yes, that's mine, and so is $3500 I have in my pocket, and a thousand acres of wheat and 500 hogs back in Iowa. You guys think I'm daffy; well, maybe I am, but I'm down here having a helluva lot of fun, that you big leaguers are providing. S'long, Tigers!"

And with that he swung into the big car and slid it into gear and drove off!

I do not mean to convey the idea that gentlemen with slightly daffy reasons for their actions are confined to the ranks of training-camp crashers. You get them on all ball clubs, yes, even on championship teams. I remember one player very well. He was a young man inclined to disappear on various occasions whenever he felt in the mood. On one road trip this particular man failed to observe a rule requiring all players to be in their hotel rooms at midnight.

The following morning I set out on a diligent search, but the player was not to be found. About noon I decided to go out to the ball park, and upon entering the clubhouse, much to my surprise, I found him engaged in a game of cards with some teammates. He had his back to the door and I walked over and touched him on the shoulder, inquiring of him:

"Where were you last night?"

Without batting an eye or uttering a word he continued with the game. Once again in a harsher tone I said:

"Where were you last night?"

After a few minutes of deep thought he turned around and said:

"I do not choose to reveal my whereabouts."

This crack broke up the meeting, as the other players took a quick runout to conceal their laughter.

So, if you want to be a ball player maybe you will finish up being a manager and having athletes give you reasons like that, and pass them off as intelligent.

Let's pass over the manager's headaches for the present and try to take apart some of the common faults of a rookie. There's more fun and less trouble in that!

II

WHAT MAKES A PLAYER

THE fundamentals that go to make a successful ball player are the same that go to make a sound athlete in any sport—knowledge of the rudiments of the game, an ability to execute plays instinctively, and a positive belief in your ability to do the latter.

The last-named essential, of course, is what we call confidence, and I know of no better way for a ball player to acquire confidence than to achieve absolute mastery of the fundamentals of the game, so that he can play first base, or hit, or catch or pitch exactly as if everything he does is the most natural thing in life.

In my own experience, for example, I was a pretty bad catcher until that day on my first spring training trip when, for no apparent reason, I began to catch naturally. My confidence improved immediately, and soon I was playing the game without regard to the things I had formerly remembered to do only by conscious effort.

Of course, no baseball coach or manager can tell a fellow like Babe Ruth or Ty Cobb how to hit; but they are the rare exceptions in the game. That they are rare is evident enough from the fact that there has been but one of each. It would be ridiculous to say that there will never be another, but when a second Ruth or Cobb comes along he will stand out above the rank and file just as they did.

These men were known for their hitting exploits. The first fundamental of hitting is to set yourself into a comfortable stance at the plate and never lose sight of the ball! There are dangers in taking your eye off the ball, danger of injury, and, worse still, danger of relaxing and taking base hits for granted; do that, and soon you are under- or over-striding and very quickly find yourself in the throes of a slump in which you can't buy a base hit with a board off the side of a barn.

Batting slumps are the bane of a ball player's existence, and about as pleasant as an income-tax blank or the threat of a truant officer over a small boy's head. At some time or other all ball players meet "Miss Slump" in person. Base hits become as alien as beef stew in the tropics.

Line drives that were base hits begin to go directly at fielders. Bats get blamed: they suddenly become too heavy or too light. Then comes the stage of experiment. The batter commences to fool with his stance. He changes the position of his feet or his arms. He believes they are too close to his body. He develops a hitch in his swing. Then comes complete loss of confidence.

He will try bunting, drag bunting, anything that is different or looks as if it might lead to a base hit.

One rule I always followed as a manager— never to fool with the batting style of a recruit until he had been up on the major leagues at least one year. My precedent for this was Mr. Mack himself, certainly a successful manager. There is nothing that will confuse a good young hitter quicker than a lot of criticism of his style. It will throw him off stride, cause him to lose confidence, and absolutely convince him that he must do something different in the major leagues from what he did in the minors.

Al Simmons was one of the greatest illustrations of this. He was passed up by more scouts than enough because he batted with his "foot in the bucket" so-called. His unorthodox style was hard to overcome in the minds of the scouts. Mack finally bought him and he reported to training camp.

Simmons asked Mack, on the first day in camp, if he wanted him to change his stance at the plate.

"How did you hit in the American Association, Al?" Connie asked him.

Al replied that he had always hit his own style.

"That's all right with me, son," said Connie;

"you can stand on your head up there—if you can hit them as often."

Dick Porter overstayed his minor league career seven years because of a double hitch in his swing, and then, he complains, after he got a trial and was successfully hitting big league pitching, he got a lot of unsolicited advice from .220 hitters on "how to get that hitch" out of his swing. But Porter did all right, finishing his major league career well over .300.

When a batter is hitting well he may lengthen or shorten his stride without its having an appreciable effect on his timing. But as soon as his batting average begins to fall off he will invite trouble by overstriding.

Ty Cobb always said that most batting slumps are caused by the feet—either by overstriding or by neglecting the position of the feet in the batting box.

Eddie Collins once, in the midst of a slump, couldn't get a base hit with the trunk of a tree. Day after day he went to the plate and came back to the dugout with another horsecollar.

One day in absolute disgust he grabbed a

fungo bat and walked up to the plate. This particular stick was used for hitting flies to the outfield and was only about an inch and a half in diameter. Collins waggled the abbreviated weapon at the opposing pitcher and slammed the first offering into left center for a base hit. Instantly his confidence returned and he was off on a hitting streak that was as thrilling as his slump had been depressing.

Ball players, like everybody else, look for a new road out of a slump once they get in the rut. But there are no signposts that point the way out of the detour.

Charley Gehringer pulled the funniest remark I ever heard from a fellow in a slump. Now, Charlie was not exactly a gabby fellow. He'd speak to you in the spring and say goodbye in the fall, with daily nods of the head. He never told anybody how good he was, and never thanked anybody for flattery.

Like that other great idol of Detroit, Cobb, Gehringer performed on the field. Cobb never let anybody doubt his ability, but he lived up to his billing. Charley just kept quietly on his way.

He'd been to bat about twenty times without getting on base, and in his last eight or ten times couldn't get the ball out of the infield. He went up for the twenty-first time against a "cunny-thumb" pitcher and slugged a pop-up deep to the pitcher's box.

"Charley," said one of the boys as Gehringer came back to the bench, "you sure mashed that one."

"I couldn't get a hit in an elevator shaft," snapped the Tiger batting star.

Players try anything to get out of a slump. They'll change bats until they are black in the face! They won't change bats before the wood cracks! They'll take extra batting practice! They'll take none at all! They try to refuse fielding practice! They'll practise until they're overtired at game time! There are any number of things they'll try, but there's still only one cure. Pick out a good ball and keep swinging!

But getting back to what makes a player: there is nothing to baseball but pitching, hitting, and throwing. All you need are good legs, a good arm, near-perfect vision, and coordination. Because, fundamental knowledge and all notwithstanding, anything can, and does, happen in baseball.

The White Sox were leading the Athletics by two runs and it was the eighth inning. The bases were filled to overflowing with nobody out. Frank Welch, on second base with the winning run, for no reason at all decided to steal third, and did. Much to his surprise, he found the base occupied when he got there and was thrown out. One out!

The next hitter batted a ball to the third baseman, and this worthy calmly threw out the runner at first base, permitting the tying run to score and the winning run to go to second. The third baseman of the Sox thought there were two out. Joe Hauser promptly singled home the winning run. Anything can happen in baseball.

Besides the hitting, throwing, pitching and fielding, I would say that the one thing which makes a player stand out above the average and pushes him toward a big league career is that poise and assurance which is carried by a confident athlete. Dizzy Dean, for example, when he was in his greatest glory. J. Hannah knew he was good and let everybody and anybody interested know he was.

When a youngster hits the big leagues there is a pat question that he's always asked: "What difference do you find between the major and minor leagues?" If he is a pitcher, he answers, "It is much easier to pitch up here. Those guys bring down anything that's hit in the park, and throw out runners from shortstop to first on blows that would go for hits in the minors."

All the youngsters exaggerate, of course. But they are instantly struck, when they get to a big league training camp, by the smooth work in the field of the big leaguer. Few of them ever look behind this smooth work to see what makes it go.

There is more than confidence. Confidence, of course, plays a part, but contributing to the natural ability, the adroit footwork, the good throwing, the accurate fielding, there is the great essential of observation.

"Keep your eyes and ears open" is one of the soundest bits of advice a young fellow ever got. Watch your own teammates and try to copy the actions of the stars.

So much emphasis has been put on power that we are inclined to overlook the fact that baseball is still a percentage game. You do certain things to meet certain developments of the contest at hand, and more often if you follow the percentage it will work to your advantage over the long run.

The reason why the youngsters taking part in a ball game with big leaguers for the first time notice the marked difference, is that the big leaguer knows what the percentage is, and is usually playing it.

One way a youngster can make himself like a big leaguer is to watch the batsmen on his own team while they are at bat. Not only will he be able to pick out the strong points of the good hitters, but by comparing them with the weaker hitters he may discover a weakness of his own and correct it.

In fielding, shifting of the feet comes to the adroit athlete naturally after he has awakened to the realization that comfort and stance go hand in hand. Certainly Charley Gehringer, one of the greatest second basemen of all time, is not a blazing beacon of color at the keystone sack, but for rock-ribbed defensive work at that position you'll look long and forlornly for a better man. Charley does it through perfect co-ordination—added, of course, to his brilliant baseball mind.

Charley was always away with the crack of the bat. By getting the jump on the ball, base hits were turned into easy outs by Gehringer.

Accurate throwing is one of the important fundamentals of the game. A good arm can sometimes compensate for the lack of speed of foot or the slowing up process which overcomes all infielders sooner or later.

Throwing is like shooting a pistol, you must keep practising to make perfect! An infielder or outfielder must practise getting the ball away from him with the greatest speed possible. Watch the speed and accuracy of a good double play combination in getting rid of the ball. The speed and timing are the essential elements of a championship player.

The infield throw is performed with a fast, snap action in which the wrist plays an important part. The infielder must learn to throw from any position—and throw accurately. A scatter-armed infielder can cause almost as much trouble as a "George Stallings pitcher."

The throw from the outfield must be made with a full arm motion so that the ball will carry swiftly to the target. Quickness in getting the throw away is, of course, an important feature, but it must not be gained at the sacrifice of power and accuracy.

An outfielder cannot throw off balance. He must get position on the ball and be ready for the throw before he makes the catch. Get behind the ball and field it coming in, whenever possible, but do not charge it!

Never take your eye off the batter, whether you are an infielder or an outfielder!

WHAT MAKES A PLAYER

Getting position on the ball is always safe advice. To get it, an outfielder must have his eye on the ball all the time. Even while his pitcher is winding up he must have his mind on that little white ball in the hurler's hand which the hurler is trying to hide from the batter. The outfielder must never let the pitcher hide it from him.

When a club takes on a new hurler, one of the first things the clever outfielder will do is to watch the newcomer's windup and delivery and follow it through. He does this so that when the ball is hit he will be able to follow it from the time it is struck by the bat.

Again we have the feet and the comfortable stance which allows the outfielder to take off in either direction as the ball leaves the bat. The toughest assignment any manager ever had is to get the outfielders to throw the ball to the infield correctly. You'll hear a critic say that Gus Recruit is a swell hitter and quite a fielder, but unfortunately he throws to the wrong base too often.

Leftfielders should always throw to the plate

low so that an infielder can cut off the throw
for a relay to the plate, or a throw to another
base to prevent an added run from getting in
scoring position. Centerfielders are prone to
make too many throws to the plate to cut off
runs, thereby permitting a hitter to take that
extra base to which he is not entitled. Right-
fielders should never make a throw to third
base so that the shortstop stands no chance of
cutting it off. The throw should be low; not too
low to affect the flight of the ball, but suffi-
ciently low so that the infielders can cut it off
and hold the hitter to first.

Naturally all of these throws depend a great
deal on the speed of the hit to the outfield,
whether the hit-and-run was on when the hit
was made, and whether the run going around
to third base—in the case of the rightfielder
making the toss—is a run of sufficient importance to gamble against another one getting
into tallying position.

Obviously, the conclusion is that the feet are
of almost first importance to the catcher, infielder or outfielder. It is just as true that an

outfielder must put emphasis on his stance and position when fielding a ball and getting ready to make a throw as the catcher or any of the men on the inner line of defense.

Shifting the feet, taking that extra step which novices are prone to make—also good outfielders with extra strong arms, at times—all add to the motions through which a fielder must go to get a throw away. And if he makes the catch, the shift and throw with a minimum of motions, it stands to reason that his throw will be there as soon as, or sooner than, the strong-arm guy who takes the extra step, and a lot quicker than the awkward fellow who must shift his feet into position before he lets the throw get away.

The benefits from good balance were never more clearly demonstrated to me than by a throw Joe DiMaggio made against Detroit when he was a freshman in the big leagues. It was the greatest throw I ever saw. In it he overcame the fact that he could not get position on the ball, and he disregarded the percentage—

and his accuracy and willingness to gamble won an important ball game for the Yankees.

The Tigers were the World's Champions. We were playing the Yankees in their own park with first place still in question. In the ninth inning we staged a rally. With one out, Pete Fox got on base and Marvin Owen singled him to third. The tying run was in scoring position and Owen was the winning run on first. Rogell hit a drive to left field. It was a sharp hit which appeared strong enough to give Detroit the tying run. DiMaggio made a fine running catch of the ball, taking it over his left shoulder. He wheeled in one motion and cut loose with a throw that carried on the fly to Dickey at the plate. He had Fox out before Pete could hit the dirt, completing as nice a double play as I have ever seen. It meant the ball game.

Nine outfielders out of ten would have made the throw to second base, allowing us the tying run but keeping the winning run out of scoring position. This was the obvious percentage play as the Yanks still had their half of the inning to overcome the tie.

WHAT MAKES A PLAYER

Ed Barrow said afterward that it was one of the smartest plays he had seen in forty years of baseball. Behind its completion, Barrow did not emphasize the power of the throw. He knew DiMaggio had that—knew it before the Yankees brought him up from the Coast League. The thing which struck Barrow was the thing which impressed every baseball man who saw it. The feet and the position that the rookie sensation took on the ball. That sort of thing wins ball games!

III

LET'S LOOK AT THE LINE-UP

ONE of the axioms of baseball is that a championship team is as strong as its center line—from the catcher through the box, over second base and to center field.

"The fans," said Connie Mack, "keep their eyes on the pitcher and the batter and the fielder to whom the ball is hit. But after I know my pitcher is working all right, I keep my eyes on the catcher. For that's where the game is played—right there behind the plate."

One of the major requirements of a catcher is to instill confidence in the pitchers he is receiving. They must have absolute faith in his judgment and his ability to catch every pitch.

A catcher must foster such confidence for his ability that a pitcher can rare back and let go with his Sunday pitch, knowing that the receiver will stop it unless it is in the stands!

Sure it is a large order! But pitchers are funny persons and must be cajoled, badgered and conned along like babies, big bad wolves, or little sisters with injured feelings. So, to avoid accidents, arguments, and "runs-sauntered-in," the best advice a young catcher ever got was to expect every pitch to be a wild pitch. That's right, *expect every pitch to be a wild pitch!*

I haven't the slightest idea where I first heard that. Or, for that matter, whether I ever heard it. Regardless of whether it is my own or some other person's, it is a sound and sane formula for catching. To my mind it is the secret of good catching. The fellow who looks for everything to come down the middle can't stop those wild ones when they turn up.

Incidentally, never let a wild pitch get you down. If one gets away from you, come back and work harder. You'll get the next guy out —and that, too, goes in life or baseball.

By always looking for the worst to happen a

catcher takes the best in stride and is never caught napping when that wild pitch does come. I do not mean to take credit for this thought. Maybe Mr. Mack told it to me when I was breaking in; perhaps somebody else said it. Its practice is the difference between a good catcher and just another receiver.

Mechanically, the first thing a catcher must acquire is a wide comfortable stance behind the plate. Stand with the left foot advanced three or four—perhaps six—inches ahead of the right foot; assume a crouch that does not tighten you up and prevent you from shifting quickly.

A catcher should NOT try to stand with his feet in the same PLANE. By standing with one foot behind the other he can shift his balance with agility, eliminating wasted motion for receiving or throwing.

The difference between a wide comfortable stance and an awkward one means as much as three full seconds with a man on base, and if he's a fast man that means ten to twenty feet—a put-out or a stolen base.

By assuming the stance that fits best, a receiver should shift his feet, catch, and throw in no more than two or three motions . . . shift, catch, throw. A clumsy fellow will require at least four motions to get the throw away, and if the man on base happens to be a speed boy he's apt to come right through and steal second, third, and your mask before you wind up.

Bases in the majority of cases are stolen on pitchers! In justification of the hurlers in the American League, at least, I can say with some authority that it is not always necessary for them to hold men on base.

In the American League the practice is to forget that one run, because the sluggers behind you will get a hatful for you if one scores. Sure, it is unsound; but it's there, and those big bats around the circuit do get those single runs back for the pitchers, and therefore you can hardly blame them for not having the proper respect for a single run.

For this reason alone it is doubly important that a catcher put all of his first thoughts into stance behind the plate. He must have his feet ready to shift easily and quickly because the old adage that there is no answer to a home run has taken hold of the entire baseball world. And, as long as this holds true, pitchers with good movements toward base runners will get fewer and fewer. I could see them going as the emphasis went more and more to the hitters during my career as a catcher. A fast catcher can overcome some of the shortcomings of slow pitchers.

One of the important requirements of a catcher is a good arm. His control is almost as important as a pitcher's. The first throw to master is to second base, the most frequently stolen station.

In making his throw the catcher calls again on his comfortable and easy stance. At ease he can pivot on his right foot, stepping directly toward second base. The throw is aimed just above the pitcher's waist line and executed with a direct overhand throw. It is practised until it becomes a mechanical movement.

There is danger for the pitcher in the throw, but with men on base—especially a known fast man—the pitcher is alive to the fact that the runner is less dangerous on first than on second and will exercise some caution in keeping him there. Better movements toward a runner than most pitchers possess would facilitate matters in holding runners to first, so in lieu of this seemingly lost art of the game, the second best thing is a fast catcher with a good arm. And he can still only cut down the liberties if the pitcher is a gross violator of the book concerning holding runners on base.

One item, however, of which the pitcher should always be careful, cropped out in a game with the Tigers when I was catching for the Athletics. George Earnshaw was pitching, and George was inclined to be a little lenient with base runners.

If a runner is in motion when a pitcher delivers the ball he should think then and there of himself—and duck!

If he stopped his motion and threw to get the runner it would be a flagrant balk. But George continued his delivery. I let go with a throw, and George, who had failed to drop to the mound with the pitch, was smacked on the back of the head. He was knocked cold.

The accident may have been responsible for the loss of the game. Earnshaw was forced to leave the game when he regained consciousness —and ultimately we lost the game.

When a play at the plate is indicated, the catcher steps in front of the plate between the batters' boxes and assumes a narrow comfortable stance which will permit him to drop to either knee, to protect the plate. The aim is to force the runner to slide around you, either to the left or right. The catcher never moves away from the plate unless his vision to the fielder making the play is blocked.

When the catcher is forced to make a diving play at the plate, he should always dive for the plate rather than at the runner, keeping in mind the necessity of blocking the plate with some part of the body. Make the runner come to you instead of your going after him and perhaps finding yourself fooled by the cleverness of a good slider. If you go for the runner instead of the plate you open yourself to a feint, somewhat like a prize fighter.

No one has yet made a put-out without the ball. So never take your eye off the ball to look at the runner. Make certain that you have possession of the ball and then keep it in the glove whenever possible. When you can make a put-out with two hands, do it. This practise will cut down on the chances of having a smart base runner kick the ball out of your bare hand.

A few years ago in Boston Jojo White, a master of the scissors kick, gave a startling demonstration of kicking a ball around. He scored from first base on an attempt to steal second.

Jojo was out by five feet at second base, but the infielder dropped his hand on a one-handed tag and White lashed out with his scissors slide and kicked the ball into left field. Up jumped White. He took off for third. Here again he was apparently out by a full stride. The play at third base was just like the one had been at second, the ball rolling over to the Detroit dugout. Jojo leaped up out of the dirt and set sail for the plate. The ball beat him to the pay station by ten feet and he went into his slide again. This time the catcher went after him, but the result was the same as it had been at second and third. He scored from first after being put out three different times.

When there is a run coming home from second base on a single which can be fielded and returned to the plate, and the marker is of paramount importance to your ball game, there is no time for a quick glance at Emily Post to decide which is the proper way to handle the runner, for his only thought is to beat that throw, and he'll do almost anything to accomplish it.

There's nothing in the rules which says he must not do anything to hinder your catch or your tagging of him. Don't be a sucker! Expect the base runner to try one kick anyway. Grip the ball tightly whenever you are going to tag a man, whether you are a catcher or an infielder. And when you have gripped it and are ready to make the dive for the plate, do not worry about where you are going to tag— tag him, put the ball on him. Beware, if you can, of flying spikes by tagging him on the legs instead of the soles of his shoes—but if that's the only place you can make the put-out, do it.

The catcher must get *in front* of every throw! With catlike leaps and bounds he must be in front of everything that comes his way. If he is crouched on his toes in a comfortable stance, always with that wild pitch on his mind, those pitches that cut the middle, the hook that breaks where it should, or the change of pace that lazes up to the plate will all come easy— right into his possession. By being in front of every pitch the receiver can cut down his passed balls, and it helps him to dig those wild pitches out of the dirt.

Remember that foul fly. It can be very embarrassing, just as it was to Frank King; remember him, back in Dover? In getting under a foul fly, keep the elements in mind—the wind and the sun. Take the force of the wind into consideration, and always be ready to protect your eyes from the sun. My plan was to shield my eyes by putting the mitt up over my head in the

49

path of the sun before I looked up to sight the ball.

Practice in the various parks in which you play will acquaint you with the distance from the plate to the backstop. Part of your job is to keep that distance in mind, to have your mind on the wind and the effect it will have on the drop of the ball, and to protect your eyes from the sun.

You'll always find that the good catcher is the one who learns never to lose sight of the ball. He watches it as it goes off the bat and follows its course in a straight line—still the shortest distance between two points. By keeping your eye on the ball you can avoid circling around under the ball. By throwing the mitt quickly across the path of the eyes you keep the glare of the sun from blinding you as you tear back for a foul fly. It helps to accommodate the eyes to the glare and prevents blinking. If the sun does blind you and you blink, you have lost that one. You might just as well give up and start back to the plate and put on your mask, because the toughest thing in the world is to pick a falling ball out of the glare of a sun that has blinded you.

In regard to the wind against a high back-stop, such as you find in big-league ball parks: the high fly will be carried by the draft, wind or not, diagonally back toward the diamond. You must allow for this. As for flies hit high above the stands, never give them up too soon. The very ball you are certain will fall into the stands out of your reach is the one that will come down in an oblique line into the park and fall, uncaught, to give a batter a life he doesn't deserve.

The toughest foul fly to handle is the sky-rocket that booms straight up into the air over the plate. There is only one way to handle it. Any other way will find the catcher running the risk of getting a fractured skull, or at least missing the catch by a foot. One sure way is to run back from the plate and come in on the ball as it begins to fall.

I once watched such a ball go up off a bat in Shibe Park when I was with the A's and knew it was ticketed for the sky. I took one look at it and walked fifteen or twenty feet back from the plate, looked up again, and it seemed to be hanging off a cloud a mile high in the air. I took my eyes off it again and stepped a few feet farther away from the plate and sighted it again. It was coming down and I waited for it to set its course. Then I ran in toward the diamond and took it on the run directly over home plate. Had I stood at the plate I never would have caught it.

You'll usually be short on a high fly, too, if you sight it and try to aim a low glove at it. Put your glove over your head and sight the ball to hit you squarely on the forehead. It's the same theory as a blocking back in football. If the blocker finds he's having trouble cutting a certain fellow out of a play by aiming his shoulder at a vulnerable spot, he will switch his sights and direct his head right at the slick fellow's middle. By that process he will hit the man's legs with his shoulder, thereby accomplishing the block which he was missing.

The dangers of injury in smashing into a wall are also like those of a blocking back in football. If the blocker hits his block with a tense drive behind him, he'll get up sore and possibly with a broken bone or two. He must deliver the blow completely relaxed at the impact. He relaxes somewhere between the time he puts the last ounce of drive into his block and the time of impact.

It is just like that with a catcher going back after a high foul. The wall is somewhere near at hand. Another three or four steps and he has position on the ball, but the wall is there, too. Should he stop, reconnoiter, take his eyes off the ball and look at the wall and then try to resight the ball? Not if he wants to make the put-out! He sets himself for the impact and tears right after the ball, never taking his eyes from it. Often, after he makes the catch, he will discover that there is ample room for another step or two in which to slow down before he bangs into the wall. Even if he does run into the wall, the worst thing that can happen is a slight banging up, bruises and the like, if he is completely relaxed like a blocking back in football.

I do not mean, of course, to be suggesting

that fellows go running around back of the plate after foul flies like men who don't care whether or not they crack their heads. The whole secret of avoiding injury is to get the distance between the backstop and the plate firmly fixed in your mind. You can know unconsciously exactly how much room you have to spare.

Outfielders, first and third basemen should also fix those distances in their mind. They are always in danger of ramming into a wall, and many career-ending injuries have occurred because an eager fielder tore into a wall trying to make a catch.

Get position on the ball, get in front of everything that comes your way, it does not make much difference whether you're a catcher or a centerfielder. If you can get in front of everything that comes your way, you're as perfect as you can be; none of us is absolutely perfect —do the best you can. Get in front of as many chances as possible.

Infielders, of course, cannot always get in front of balls. They do not have time on line drives that whiz by like a shot. But if the infielder is ready and waiting in a comfortable stance, his feet spread, ready to drive him to the right or left, forward or to the rear in one motion, he'll stand a better chance of getting almost in front of the ball, than if he is awkwardly just standing around out there waiting for some lefty to blast one by him.

Here, too, in fielding those line drives, comes the wisdom of knowing all you can about the hitter. It is the duty of the infielder to study the hitting strength and weakness of a batter just as the battery must acquaint themselves with these fine points of the counterattack.

An infielder should always study the signs of the catcher and know as often as possible exactly what pitch is on; and he should have the hitters so catalogued in his mind that he will instantly know exactly what the man at bat will do with that sort of ball—the average number of times.

The stance, and alertness to the possibilities of the hitters, are essential factors in the success of a good fast double-play combination.

BASEBALL

If the feet and stance are important to the catcher, second baseman and infielders on the left of the diamond, they are of overwhelming importance to a first baseman. Cleverness with the feet around the opening base can avoid injury.

The toughest play for a first baseman to make is to get out of the base path and take a wild throw, removed from harm's way, in the path of a flying runner. Joe Judge and Joe Kuhel were picture performers at this. Others have never been able to master the play. Oftentimes you just can't help yourself and find that you are right in the base path, the ball almost on you and the runner bearing down with all his speed. Certainly he's not going to run around you to make a base to which he is entitled. So he bowls into you, and then it is a wild scramble with every man for himself.

Hank Greenberg found himself in such a position in a series between the Tigers and Washington Senators when Jake Powell collided with him and aggravated an injury he had suffered in the previous fall's World Series. Hank was lost for the rest of the season.

Foxx always has tried to receive the ball rather than fight it. He's a big strong fellow and has no fear of anybody coming down that base path, but it has been his experience that less trouble is confronted if the first baseman— and he played a fair third base, too—will go with the ball and the runner, also, rather than fight them. By "fighting" the ball and runner, Foxx means pushing the body or hands out to meet either.

And it is the same with every infield position. Fumbling is caused more often by charging the ball than by any other cause. As the ball comes to the infielder, he tries to receive it by bringing his hands back toward his body in the path of the ball's flight.

The only sure preventive of getting bowled over when you find yourself in the path of the runner while playing first base is to take the throw outside the diamond. By stepping out of the diamond and taking the wide throw, the first baseman avoids collision with the oncoming runner and so comes up whole and complete, and very often with the put-out.

Again the feet have it when the keystone combination is considered. The comfortable and easy stance which permits a second baseman or shortstop to shift quickly and with grace to either his right or left, will facilitate the completion of double plays, still the greatest defense measure in the old ball game.

In the American League, the smart manager will gamble a run for a double play any time. Speed of foot, accurate hands, and control of the relay throw by the player trying to complete the double killing are the items which go to make up a double play combination.

It is not my intent to say that any infielder can accomplish the adroitness of a Gehringer and master the art of going in either direction with the ease of the great Detroit second baseman by only watching his feet. But I do insist that you'll find the fellow with a weakness for going in either direction is usually a lad with an awkward and tense stance in his position waiting for the hit.

IV

DEFENSE

Pitching is the first-line defense. On the catcher falls the burden of keeping the pitcher on an even keel; of keeping his mind off danger and on the hitter, and never allowing the hurler to beat himself.

Good pitchers come in paradoxes, and it is the job of the catcher to learn the combat psychology which best fits the fellow on the mound. Two of the most confusing types are the man who gets mad and beats himself, and the man who can't do anything until he is mad.

On the great Athletics teams with which I played we had two perfect examples of these types. The great Mose Grove was a quick-tempered workman who would blow up over seemingly trivial incidents. Lefty, in his later years with Boston, had calmed down and mellowed considerably. But when he was at his peak of greatness there was nobody who could match him in invective when something had gone wrong behind him, or when I had called for the wrong pitch against his wish and he had seen it sail over the rightfield wall.

Lefty was really a good-natured fellow when the pressure of the game was off. He was a tough loser, and, for my part, I'll take that sort of competitor any time in preference to the chap who loses with a high heart.

Grove rarely kept his feelings a secret when something bothered him. He'd spout off on the field or on the bench. One day he was particularly exercised over some turn of the game and was letting off considerable steam, ending his tirade with a very unpretty and abusive climax. The effect was to make the recipient of these unkind words want to crawl into the nearest knothole until the high-pitched, angry voice of Mr. Mack—whose harshest words usually were "Ah, shucks!"—pierced the calm, repeating Lefty's identical words, all for Grove and nobody else. Even the tense and inflamed Grove almost fell off his dugout seat, as did all the others, at Mack's use of such language.

Usually, however, it is right in the heat of a game that this type chooses to blow up. It is then the concern of the receiver to calm him down, con him with a wisecrack, get his mind off the tenseness of the situation, and finally tell him that he's going to strike out the next two men. It has some effect on a pitcher of the competitive spirit of Grove.

Just the opposite of Lefty was Rube Walberg on the same club, a lackadaisical fellow who'd go along and take everything, even a homer with the bases filled, in stride unless he was mad. I'd work on Rube and get him so mad at me personally that he'd want to murder me with every pitch—in trying to take my glove off he would, incidentally, fire the ball right by a good many hitters.

The pitcher with great speed, great control or a fine hook and perfect competitive temperament can develop faults, too. Even the best of them can have something wrong when the heat of the battle is on.

The most common fault of great pitchers when they get a lead, or seemingly have the opposition fooled, is to get smart. They ease off in their efforts and try to fool smart hitters. Occasionally this type will lay up a change of pace, or a carelessly thrown pitch, right in the middle of a jam.

I'm not one and never was, to find fault with a man of courage. But when the heat is on, the percentage is against a display of courage—if courage is exemplified by taking chances with a slugger like Jimmie Foxx at the plate, the score tied, and the winning run on second base.

Hitters like Foxx, DiMaggio, Gehrig, and Ruth in his heyday, had the perfect answer to the smart-aleck hurler trying to slip over a sneak pitch on them. I remember when a fellow of this school of thought one day offered a change of pace to a slugger on the three and two pitch. The hitter represented a very important run. He took sight on the change of pace, adjusted his swing, his stance and power to meet it, and changed its pace completely. It sailed over the outfield wall and the would-be smart pitcher was chagrined at the turn of events. A ball game which appeared won was tied up and he went on to lose. Such events are not rare, actually.

Fooling sluggers is one thing to think about, but making it work is another. Once I saw Jimmie Foxx belt a ball out of Comiskey Park when the pitcher had meant it to be a waste ball. With the hit-and-run on and Tony Lazzeri at bat you'd almost have to throw the pitchout to the first baseman to get the Walloping Wop to let it go by. Al Simmons in a World Series reached out and belted one out of the park.

Which reminds me of the comment of Carl Hubbell after the 1937 World Series between the Giants and Yankees. Lou Gehrig had sailed one into the rightfield seats off Hubbell in a very tense situation.

"They talk about hitting weaknesses," said Hubbell, "why, that guy won't even take a base on balls when you give it to him. That pitch he hit into the seats was away out here." And

Carl reached his hand out as far as it would go at the level of his eyes.

There's no answer to such slugging. The only thing to bear in mind with such hitters is never to take the .250 hitter in stride. Bear down on these birds, and the pitchers. Strike 'em all out on three pitched balls if you can.

"Those big hitters are going to get so many hits anyway," Connie Mack used to say, "so do not worry about them. Get the light hitters out and pitch your best to the sluggers. The results will usually be all right."

In bearing down on the lesser lights of a batting order, the good pitcher is forever careful with the pitchers. One of the cardinal rules for pitching to pitchers is never to throw them a change of pace. Notoriously pitchers are late swingers, and a change of pace is right up their alley. They catch hold of one and, in the case of the right-handed hitting pitcher, dump it into left field for a base hit.

The way to handle pitchers is to fire three strikes right down the middle and get them out as soon and easily as possible.

DEFENSE

Mention of sluggers like Simmons, Foxx, Gehrig, Gehringer, Greenberg, York, brings up the question of the defensive strategy.

Considerable comment was stirred up by a situation in a recent World Series when Joe McCarthy of Yankees supposedly spotted the Giants a run in a situation immediately following one of the same order. The managers had used opposite tactics.

In an early inning the Yankees had men on first and third with none out, and Bill Terry called his infield in on the grass to cut off the run. The results were not gratifying, because the Yanks splurged with a rally. Within an inning or two the Yanks, in a similar situation, played the infield back, gave the Giants the run which scored, as the shortstop and second baseman and first baseman collaborated on a double play.

This is not gambling, according to the baseball played in the American League, and Joe McCarthy, a smart percentage playing manager, would be the last man to say it was. By the standards of the younger circuit this is strictly sound percentage baseball.

In the American League you must play for the big inning. If one run is going to beat you, you might as well concede the game before you leave the clubhouse. Therefore the American League's defense is to stop the big inning. In our league, often as late as the eighth inning, the strategy would be to give the opposition the tying run to cut off a rally, which might bring on a big inning.

If there was any importance in the comparisons of the McCarthy and Terry strategy in the foregoing situation, it could be that it clarified the essential difference between the two leagues. In the National League one run is apparently important. In the American League the big inning is the thing.

Over in the National League they have developed a play that seems to have gained popularity. The dangers of it would be brought home quickly in the American League if you made a practice of it.

That is the play in which the infield, with

men on first and second, plays to force a man at third base and try for the double play at second. To be successful, the pitcher must be an exceptionally good fielder. He covers the left side of the infield. The right side of the infield is covered by the first baseman as the pitch is made. The third baseman remains back on his base ready to take the throw from the pitcher or the first baseman, whichever fields the bunt.

That play may work for the managers in the National League, but in the American, where a team of sluggers is always ready to annihilate your pitcher, the percentage is always to play for the sure out. Play the bunt for certain outs first, and play for the double play whenever you can.

With the infield drawn in, a "blooper" or humpbacked liner can go for two bases and knock runs across the plate and put more in position to score. And still none out! Of course, the same thing can happen with the infield playing back in its normal positions, but the percentage is greater for a double play on a ground ball. The same ball which might scream through the infield playing on the grass may be a put-out, even at the cost of a run with the infielders back where they belong.

There is always the goal of the double play—a bigger goal, in my opinion, at which to shoot than the cutting off of a single run. For my part I'll snuff out a rally that might turn into a big inning rather than stop a lone marker from scoring.

You may always get that one run back, but if the opposition blows one pitcher off the hill and works on another you are in a jam—a jam which might have been avoided by playing the percentage. When such developments occur you can't play percentage any more for that day. Then you must take chances, switch pitchers, look to pinch hitters, take unnecessary chances, press the percentage all the way through. And it catches up in the wrong end of the score.

In the big inning, too, is the consideration of the intentional pass. In the American League, I have noticed, you will rarely find a manager ordering the tying or winning run put on base—either to get a double play or to move around a power hitter in order to get at a weaker batter.

And never, with men on first and third, move a batter to first base on an intentional pass. The best you can get out of it is right before you— a double play.

Only a few times in my career in the American League did I see tying or winning runs put on base intentionally and every time I saw those same runs lose ball games. After all, it is the base on balls which beats you more often than hits. Those runs which get on base by the shortest route possible, the free ticket, are like everything else in life that's free—they're tough to swallow.

On defense, there is perhaps no more important piece of strategy than to know the enemy hitters and play your fielders to stop them. Always remember Mack's advice, that they are going to get their percentage of hits anyway and there's nothing but a slump can stop them.

With Mack on the bench moving outfielders around with his scorecard, you had what amounted to another outfielder on the bench. He knew hitters, their weaknesses and their strength. And while he might have ordered a pitcher to pick out a slugger's weakness, he always played his defense alignment to a man's strength.

A couple of examples of this were the plans for playing Babe Ruth and Bill Dickey. In my later day, Dickey was the toughest man in the league to down when the jam was on, but in the early days of the Yankee-Athletics rivalry Babe Ruth was the most murderous man in the league with a bat in his hand.

Ruth might hit anything into the seats. You couldn't even fire a fast ball by him if he had it measured. Lefty Grove let go with one of his fireballs in a game at the Stadium. The pitch was on the outside, and I clearly remember the thought which flashed across my mind and which was completed, incidentally, in confusion.

I'd called for a fast one outside, and Lefty let it go right where it was asked; the Babe swung, there was a smack, and it was gone—

gone into the bleachers. And as Lefty let go with that pitch, I'd have sworn that no living man could pull it to right field. But the Babe did! With such a hitter there's nothing much you can do save to line up your defense to meet his strength, and pitch to his weakness.

Babe's weakness, if any, was never exactly obvious. He'd blast a pitch over the wall in one turn at bat and the very next time up he'd whiff gloriously and colorfully on the identical ball. We always tried to keep the ball close to his hands and mix up change of speeds.

Recall Mack's advice about weak hitters and good ones. The good ones are going to get so many hits anyway, so get the little fellows out and hope for the best against the sluggers. His strategy against Ruth was the perfect example of trying to find a slugger's weakness and playing your defense to his strength.

Looking for this weakness is enough to drive a manager or a catcher out of his mind. We had a fellow one time who thought he knew how to stop Gehrig. Lou was on a rampage at Shibe Park, belting out homers at every turn of the wheel. Lou had had three and was going to bat in the seventh inning, a chance to set a lifetime record of four homers in one game.

This fellow told Connie that the way to stop Gehrig was to offer him a curve, then a waste ball, a change of pace, then waste another, a fast ball, waste another, and then make him dig a hook off the outside corner. Mack smiled benignly and offered to follow the scheme. I forget which one it was, but somewhere along the way the plan went aground. Lou smashed one of the offerings over the rightfield wall for his fourth home run of the game!

Sluggers are like that. When you think you have them worried and in the hole, they pick out your best pitch and knock a plank out of the farthest fence in the outfield. Do the best you can and play your defensive alignment to meet their strength, the way they hit most often. Mack did that with Ruth.

We would shift the whole team around toward the right. The first baseman on the right field foul line, the second baseman on the grass in short rightfield midway between first and

Lefty Grove learned control and became one of baseball's greatest hurlers.

Tommy Bridges starts windup for his jug-handle curve.

*Bridges never takes his eye off the batter as he prepares
for delivery.*

Now
Tommy is
ready to let
it go. . . .
Eyes on the
batter, feet
well set
under him,
and ball
concealed
as much as
possible.

Photo courtesy
Detroit Times

The follow-through, which makes one of the toughest curves to hit in the league.

Photo courtesy
Detroit Times

One of the most effective pitchers of all time, Walter Johnson, the Senators immortal.

Photo by Sam André, Pic Magazine

*Learning to keep his eyes on the batter will help Bobby
Feller to gain control.*

Lefty Gomez, a mainstay of the Yankees' great teams, bears down with his fast ball. Note Lefty's grip on the ball, held firmly in his pitching hand.

second, the shortstop behind second base, and the third baseman in the normal position of the shortstop. The outfield moved around correspondingly.

Naturally, the set-up looked incongruous and lopsided, and it did leave a vulnerable hole big as an acre down the left field foul line; and often the Babe would choke his bat and drop one over third base for a base hit. But as far as Mr. Mack was concerned, the alignment of the defense was still good percentage baseball. Mack reasoned it was better to give him one such hit than a long hit which might send everybody to the paystation.

Holding the Babe to one base hit when he was in his heyday was a decided relief. For any time he came to bat he'd be apt to break up your ball game. The same was true of Bill Dickey in later years—one of the most dangerous hitters any pitcher was ever asked to face; a batsman capable of depositing your ball game against the rightfield wall without asking your permission.

The backbone of the defense, save the battery, is the second-base combination. Ease, grace, accurate throwing, thorough knowledge of enemy batters, good legs, speed, perfect balance, are just a few of the requirements around second base.

The plays by the book can be taught but execution is another thing. And whenever you find a championship team you will always find that second-base duet collaborating on double plays—the best play in the book. And, except when one of my side hits a triple in the park, the double play is the most exciting single development of a game.

There is a routine for assigning the men to take throws at second base.

With a curve ball being thrown to a right-handed hitter, the second baseman will take the throw. Under normal conditions the right-handed hitter will pull a curve ball to left field and hit late on a fast ball. In the event of a fast ball the shortstop takes the throw and the second baseman covers his own territory.

There are some exceptions to this. When a batter is known to be a pull hitter the combination works accordingly. For example the second baseman always covers the throw when a batter like Foxx is at the plate, or other such power hitters whose strength is in left field. And the shortstop covers on all dead right-field hitters.

The second-base combination is one which must work in absolute harmony. One player must complement the other. Of course you'll get an ordinary shortstop who can be made to look good with a great second baseman and vice versa. But where you have youth, balance, speed, good hands, accurate and strong throwing arms, you'll find that a championship team is in the making.

The great teams of all time have all had great double-play combinations. . . . Tinker-to-Evers-to-Chance, Barry-to-Collins-to-McGinnis, Boley-Bishop-Foxx, and Peckinpaugh-Harris-Judge.

Throwing to the wrong base can have a disastrous effect on a young man's big league career. One of the most common errors made by rookie outfielders is not getting the ball back to the infield, and quickly, whether or not it is the right base to which they throw. Seasoned players will sometimes tempt a fast base runner to stretch a hit by making a motion as if to throw to the base he has just reached, seeking to make the fast man commit himself. But the wise base runner is not often fooled.

The one point to bear in mind in throwing from the outfield is to get the ball back to the infield. Never try to get smart and pick a man off who has overrun first, unless you are quite certain that he has left himself open. Then the danger of a throw to first for the pickoff is that the runner has overrun first not only too far to get back but far enough to make a break for second and to reach the keystone sack before the first baseman can relay a throw to that base. In such cases the safest—and percentage—play is to get the ball back at once to second base. On a two-baser to left, get the ball to the third baseman; to left center, to the shortstop or third baseman; to right center, to the second baseman, and in rightfield to the second baseman on the grass or the first baseman near the mound.

DEFENSE

The throws from the outfield should always be made low enough to be cut off. The shifting of the players on hits to the outfield is also of prime importance. What single player is definitely out of the play on a hit to the outfield? And where is he of most efficient use?

The answer is, the first baseman. And his most effective position is near the pitcher's mound. From that point he can take directions from the catcher on the progress of the play, watch the throw from the outfield, and relay the information from the catcher to the other infielders or cut off the throw himself and relay the ball to another base for a play, or hold the ball and stop the runners from taking too many liberties.

A feature of the defense demands on-your-toes baseball in the backing-up plays—all plays. First is the catcher. An alert and fast catcher can avoid trouble by hustling down to back up first base on a fast double play. For it is the fast twin killing where the man relaying the throw to first base sometimes is forced to make the peg while he is off balance.

BASEBALL

Waiting to land on the ground and regain balance on your feet may mean a perfect throw, but it will mean fewer twin outs.

The man at second base making the throw has to watch himself that he doesn't get knocked into the left field seats by the forced runner barging into him and breaking up the play. The runner is not going to get out of your way. Remember what happened to Dizzy Dean in that series with Detroit? He got hit by a relayed pitch smack on the forehead.

The man making the relay must first watch himself; then, and next, comes the runner. The only interest in him is to see that he does not get in the way of the throw. So in getting around the base runner between first and second the second baseman or shortstop is many times off balance when he makes the throw.

Speed is the heartbeat of a double play. And a fast catcher who can move down behind first base to back up the play is insurance against the hitter gaining too much ground if the peg is bad and error results.

He should cover third base when the third

baseman has to handle a bunt and cannot get back to his base. The base can be gained by a base runner without a protesting gesture if the catcher does not get down there and cover it.

In backing up bases, the most important factor is the anticipation of the play. For example, any time a play at the plate is indicated, the pitcher takes up his position, and in a hurry, behind the catcher. Prompt backing up the catcher will save a pitcher future trouble if he anticipates a misplay at the plate and is ready to retrieve a fumbled ball for the catcher, thereby preventing further scoring in the event one run does get in.

On throws from right or center field, with no play at the plate suggested, the pitcher should hightail it over behind the third baseman. It is sometimes hard for the *"Spaulding Guide"*—every move a picture—type of pitcher to hustle when a rally is choking his stuff out of him. The catcher must keep after this fellow, yelling at him and driving him to give a little more in his participation than throwing the ball and looking pretty doing it.

BASEBALL

Backing up third base and the plate, a pitcher can help prevent a lot of trouble. Oftentimes a misplay at one of these bases will develop into a retired runner where but a few seconds before this same runner looked mighty like a run.

For example, a third base coach with a gambling spirit may chase a runner going into third and on home when a catcher loses a throw from the outfield in a vain attempt to get a runner ahead of the fellow at third. The coach is gambling on the pitcher's nervousness in such a situation, depending on the confused hurler to make a wild throw. Good fielding pitchers rarely oblige.

With men on base when a rundown pops up there are a couple of ways of killing off the runners. The success of the Yankees with a daring piece of strategy in rundowns has confused many experts.

For example, the Yanks, with a man on third attempting to score on an infield chance, will whip the ball to the catcher who often will make two throws to get the runner.

DEFENSE

It is unorthodox because the runner during the rundown is twice chased toward the next base. The catcher takes the throw from the infielder and chases the runner back toward third base. And here the third baseman does the unorthodox, he chases the runner toward the plate. The efficiency of the play depends upon the third baseman timing his throw to the plate so that when he takes the second throw from the catcher he will be close enough to tag the runner and get off a throw to second base for a play there.

The safest way in rundowns, of course, is to make one throw. The fielder relays to the catcher and he chases the runner back toward third and only throws the ball if he can't catch him. The play often occurs so fast that the hitter cannot round first and make a safe break for second. And if he does there is very often time to make a play on him. Anyway, the defense is pretty certain of getting one man by making the play in this fashion. The way the Yanks make it, on occasions, they get two—and in recent years they've been getting two almost as many times as they get one.

The run-up is a play in which the outfielders must be just as alert as the infielders. They must be on their toes and back up the infielders in the event of wild throws or the ball hitting the runner and going wild.

Finally, on defense there is the infielder who takes it for granted that the other fellows will do his work for him. That would be the average pitcher. There are few pitchers—and they are getting fewer—who can field their positions. When you had fellows like Ed Rommel and Ted Lyons working on the mound the old Athletics and the White Sox had a fifth infielder. Today, however, the pitchers cover first because an alert infielder or catcher will yell at them to "get over there," and they field a slow roller or bunt for the same reason.

When McCarthy came to the American League, he inaugurated a practice which he had used in the American Association and the National League. It is an effective drill, for in addition to making the pitchers hustle on the

DEFENSE

mound in their fielding duties it also helps put flabby hurlers into condition. I adopted the drill with Detroit and found it effective in both directions. It is a simple device and can be employed with a rookie catcher and a fellow named Joe on first base.

You line up the pitchers back of the rubber. A pitcher makes a throw to the plate, simulating a pitch to an imaginary hitter, and the catcher rolls out a bunt in front of the plate which the pitcher has to field and throw to the base called by the catcher. It is a drill that will put pitchers on their toes!

V

BATTING!

WHEN I was breaking into baseball I knew I could do one thing. I could hit. My speed and adaptability I knew would help, but the one thing that I had which nobody could take away from me was that I could hit. That, I felt, would carry me along until I rounded off the edges.

I wasn't the only ball player who was rough on the edges but could hit. The Yankees have a young fellow on whom they broke some of their chain-store rules.

Oscar Vitt, the manager of the Newark farm of the Yankee chain, had an outfield which he thought was set. But the Yankees were looking ahead to 1939 and '40 and saw the need of a left-handed power hitter. They picked this fellow from their various chattels and shipped him from a college campus to the Newark training camp at Sebring, Florida.

Now Ole Os Vitt is no different from any other seasoned manager. He could not fancy a college outfielder breaking up his season's plans. He accepted the young fellow and gave him a uniform. He watched the kid go to the plate in batting practice. The kid took a cut, there was a resounding smack of wood on leather, and the ball sailed over the center field fence—the first time the feat had been accomplished.

In spite of his background of college baseball and a failing for doing the wrong thing in the field, the young fellow stayed with the fast-stepping Newark club through a tough double-A baseball season and led the league in hitting. He batted over .350 in his second year and was a good bet to cause Yankee regulars concern in the future. The college kid was Charley Keller!

Back in the days when I was a youngster getting ready for a baseball career, there was a pitcher and an outfielder with Columbia University, who would pitch or play the outfield, or first base on occasions. However that may be he was always in the line-up, for he could belt that old apple over the fence. The name was Lou Gehrig.

"He's not good enough as a pitcher," said the cagey Miller Huggins, "and besides, a fellow who hits like that is needed every day. But he's not fast enough for the outfield."

Nobody would have given up on Gehrig, least of all the wiley Huggins. Lou was farmed out to Hartford, where he was instructed in the ways and means of playing first base; and I guess he did all right. He took over the job from Wally Pipp in 1925 and never was moved off the base for an entire game through fourteen seasons, breaking all records for uninterrupted playing.

Hank Greenberg was a similar problem to the Detroit club. He was made into a first baseman and seems to be doing all right. His big bat was needed for daily work.

Rudy York, one of the major problems in

my last season at the helm of the Detroit club, was tried in almost every position. We tried him, after a spell of catching, in the outfield. Harry Cross, one of the better baseball writers, described Rudy's truck with a fly ball in this fashion: "York does not catch a fly, he surrounds it." So we put Rudy back behind the plate.

I'll never forget the first day I told him he was to be a catcher. He didn't believe me. He thought he was going to have a try at it, fail and go back to the bushes. He'd played first base some in the minors, but he couldn't move Greenberg out of that position.

I told Rudy to get behind the bat and catch.

"What are you trying to do, kid me?" he asked.

But when he saw that I was serious, he became firm. He said he didn't like to catch. I told him, if he wanted to sit on the bench, that was all right with me. But the only way he was ever going to break into our line-up was as a catcher. I guess he thought to himself that that would be breaking into a line-up in disguise, but he did it anyway. And even if he was no ball of fire right off the mark, we had his big bat in action, and in August of the first year we experimented with him he beat Babe Ruth's record for home runs hit in one month. And for a fellow with the limited experience York had, he did all right.

You can afford to experiment with a long-range hitter of the type of York; and, yes, sometimes you can overlook fielding weaknesses. Scouts are looking for batters. Mike Gonzales, sent to scout, wired his boss, turning thumbs down on the prospect in these words: "Good field, no hit." That ended the prospect's prospects, as far as Mike was concerned.

Even pitchers like to hit. Lefty Gomez does more talking about his hitting than his pitching—which is passable in any league. They tell me that Lefty's reaction to the spectrum-yellow baseball, now an optional ball in some leagues, was that it must be a good ball: "I hit it against the fence, didn't I?"

Gomez is not alone in his thirst for base hits. Everybody wants to hit. Even the experts are

Rogers Hornsby, whose right-handed batting form has been imitated, but never very successfully. One of the greatest of all time.

Photo by Sam André, Pic Magazine

Jimmie Foxx, considered by his former teammate, the author, to be the greatest slugger of them all.

Mule Haas, a dependable hitter, a good guy around a ball club when the A's were riding high.

Jimmie Dykes was an inspirational force as well as a good hitter with that great A's team of '29.

Ironman Lou Gehrig in an action shot revealing the source of his great power.

Hank Greenberg, power hitter of the championship Tigers.

Joe DiMaggio destined to be one of the game's greatest attractions.

Cobb still the greatest of 'em all.

partial to hitters. Look back through the list of Most Valuable Player awards and you find such names as George Sisler, Babe Ruth, Lou Gehrig, Al Simmons, Joe Cronin, Foxx, Greenberg, DiMaggio, all of them hitters.

The hold on public interest was never better brought home to me than during the winter when I was sold by Portland to the Athletics. Of course, the homefolk in Boston could not know whether I was a passably good catcher or not. I alone knew I wasn't—that is, around Boston.

During the winter I visited a newspaper office—after the purchase of my contract was announced by Philadelphia.

"Do you think you'll be able to hit that pitching in the American League?" was the question which I answered at least five times on that visit. I replied that I thought I would. I thought the pitching distance was the same in the American League as it had been in the Pacific Coast League, and that up there they played with a ball and I had a bat. I felt pretty confident of my ability to hit, but later I got

the best advice a youngster was ever given—
the same by Tyrus Raymond Cobb.

"Get out in front of every pitch," he advised. "Always swing looking for a fast ball.
If you are set for speed there will be time to
hit a curve, and lots of time to set yourself for
a change of pace or slow ball!"

Cobb's secret of success as a hitter was his
marked ability to get out in front of the pitch.
He always looked for the fast ball. He was on
his own, taking signs from nobody. He never
took a pitch for granted. He was ready for the
fireball, and able to adjust his swing for a curve
or change of pace. He took good care of almost
everything that came his way; often enough, at
least, to win a place in the hall of fame of baseball as long as the game is played.

The first thing you heard when you were a
kid playing in the back lots was, "It only takes
one to hit it, kid, come on, belt it out." It's still
the same, it only takes one to hit it; and has
since Abner Doubleday laid out the first diamond. The rules, the field, the ball, the technique, all have changed, but it still only re-

quires one good look, one good pitch, and one good swing to make a base hit—or a home run.

Pick out a good one and hit it! Keep swinging!

To accomplish this a hitter must have patience. He can control his swing and develop his patience to come through with his best swing when he gets the ball he likes best. Naturally, a pitcher is trying to avoid giving you the ball you'll murder.

Patience will keep him coming through as long as you can make him throw them. It can get embarrassing when you suddenly find yourself with three and two on you where a moment before you had the pitcher in the hole at three and nothing. But circumstances are not all against you. Sure you must hit! But the pitcher must come through with a good pitch, and if his control is sagging, you'll find that the pressure is worse on him than it is on you.

Young players frequently are fooled by bad balls. They go for pitches over their heads or in the dirt; some even have been known to try to get wood on a pitch behind their own backs.

BASEBALL

There have been cases where bad-ball hitters have been good, but the percentage is against it. Hitting at bad balls comes from two things. Cause No. 1 is trying to outguess the pitcher, thereby making a guess hitter of yourself; and at the bottom of Cause No. 2 is the habit of taking signs.

Stealing signs is a worthy practice and it has its place in a ball game, but for a hitter to rely entirely upon information from a sign stealer, or allow himself to get used to being furnished with advance information on the pitch, is a very bad habit. It can cause the hitter, even the good hitter, to tighten up at the plate. If crossed up by the pitcher he's apt to go for a bad ball. In sign stealing always remember that there is no law prohibiting the other side from stealing the signs. They can learn just as you do that the sign has been stolen and change the sign while the pitcher is winding up.

In a World Series game of the '29 series with the Cubs, the Athletics knew every pitch, yet we were beaten.

Now let us leave hitting at bad balls—which

BATTING!

a hitter can overcome by never losing sight of the ball in flight or in the pitcher's hand—and pass on to the good balls. We hear all too much of the fellow who swings at the bad pitches, but precious little of the boy who swings at the best pitch.

Every pitcher has a best pitch. Let him get that out of his system, and unless it is a third strike, take it.

Take a strike. Take two strikes to get the ball you want to hit. Patience and confidence are the only attributes which will make young players do this; and of course they must decide exactly what is the best ball a pitcher throws. Naturally, if it is a fast ball, let's say, and you hit a fast ball better than any other pitch—well, what are you waiting for? Swing!

Letting strikes go by when they look good is a difficult subject to discuss with anxious players. But the great hitters are the essence of patience and confidence in waiting for the ball they want.

One of the greatest assets Charley Gehringer has is his calm in working on a pitcher. No pitcher is making Charley hit at anything he doesn't like by simply throwing that ball up there. He'll work a pitcher to three and two and never give a thought to the pressure on himself; instead of worrying about that, Charley considers that now is his big chance. The pitcher must make the next throw good, and all he needs is some wood on the ball to make a base hit.

Guess hitters rarely have such confidence. They'll murder a good one if they get it.

Cobb was the last word in confidence. He'd walk up to the plate and go through his didoes of making the plate ready with a manner that inspired fear in the hearts of opposing pitchers. And his confidence contributed to the .367 grand batting average for twenty-three years of service in baseball. He looked like a hitter and he acted like one, and to make matters worse for the opposition, he was everything he appeared to be.

Cobb would send up the hit-and-run sign with a count of two strikes and no balls on him and think nothing of it. Then he'd blast the cripple into rightfield like a shot from a cannon, the runner off with the pitch and Cobb ready to round first and tear for second if the outfielder juggled the ball or threw to get the runner at third base.

When I was a young catcher with the Athletics, Cobb was at bat one day with the count two strikes and no balls on him and he snappily informed me he was going to put on the hit-and-run.

"I'll pitch out," I told him.

"That's all right," he said. "It's on, Mickey, I'll wave to you from first base."

I signaled my pitcher for a "pitch-out" which he made. Cobb reached across the plate and slashed a single into right field on a pitch which was obviously a ball and on which I might have caught the runner who had taken off from first base. The runner went to third and Cobb waved airily at me as he trotted back to first base. All I could do was take my cap off to him—which I did.

Frank (Lefty) O'Doul, twice batting champion of the National League, was one of the most confident hitters I ever watched; and his calm, collected and serene poise at the plate in the deciding game of the Giants-Washington World Series of 1933 was one of the finest exhibitions of cold confidence I have ever seen.

Lefty went to the plate with the tying run on second base. He was confident that somewhere along the line he would get a pitch that he could murder. He wasn't looking for it right away, but he had set his mind on waiting for it. That one he was determined to hit, but definitely he had no intention of swinging at something he did not like.

Lefty was at the fag end of a picturesque career which had seen him start as a pitcher and come back as an outfielder. In that Washington-Giants series he was playing in his first World Series!

Throughout the series he'd warmed the bench. Now in the deciding game he wanted to make the most of his chance. Vanity has a place in a man's nature at such a point, and Lefty no doubt was thinking that here at the end of his career as a player in the big leagues he was at bat in the last game, an important game-winning rally under way.

He'll remember that time at bat, too. He fouled off a couple, watched a waste ball go by, and then another. He could not seem to get the one he wanted. He never got it.

"I knew I could get a hit," he said afterward, "but I was looking for a good one to lace out of the park. I never got it."

When the good one failed to come, Lefty took what he got when the chips were down and drove a single to center. The big rally went on, the tying run scored, and the Giants went on to win the ball game and the World Series.

Jimmie Foxx, Al Simmons, Lou Gehrig, and Tony Lazzeri were fellows like that. They all had supreme confidence at the plate. And that confidence is half the battle in trying to be a good hitter.

One of the things that make baseball the great fans' sport is its paradoxes. Anything can and does happen in a ball game. The confidence that a player must possess to be a good hitter is a paradox in itself.

Confidence is all right as long as it does not become overconfidence; for the good pitcher on the hill facing the good hitter should, and does, have confidence that he can whiff the good hitter.

There is no set rule that any coach or manager can lay down for working on this or that type of pitcher. The fellow inclined to be wild you will make pitch as much as possible to tire him for the late innings. If you can work this chap long and arduously every inning as the innings go by, he may weaken before his customary time and you may get him.

The control pitcher with a good fast ball and anything that passes for a fair curve, you cannot afford to wait out. This fellow comes close to being a great pitcher, and no amount of waiting for him to come to you, or getting his best pitch out of his system, will do any good.

Get him as soon as you can. Swing at anything that looks good. Keep swinging, something is sure to go sometime.

BATTING!

There was a lot of comment about the surge of the Tigers in a double header against the Yankees in the pennant race of the 1934 season. The bill was scheduled for the middle of a week in August, 1934. We were in first place by a scant margin, but the Yanks were breathing on our necks. First place hung in the balance when we took the field before a huge crowd.

Joe McCarthy led with his ace, Vernon Gomez. I sent General Alvin Crowder against him, withholding my ace, Schoolboy Rowe, for the second game. I have never believed it effective to use ace against ace. From the grandstand and crowd point of view, this is all right, but when it comes to winning games throughout the season the percentage is against it. Why sacrifice an almost certain win for a possible low-score loss? In a World Series it is a different matter; the time is too short to gamble much.

But even there you cannot say one policy is better than another. Recall that '29 series when Mr. Mack started the opening game with Howard Ehmke. I was to catch the game, and even I didn't know that Howard was to start it. Everybody, fans, writers and players alike, thought Mr. Mack had Lefty Grove warming up under the stands.

"Is *he* going to pitch?" I asked Mr. Mack when Ehmke started his warm-up.

"Yes, Mickey, he is," said the kindly old gentleman, and then with a twinkle in his eye: "He is, if it's all right with you."

"If he's good enough for you, he's good enough for me," I replied.

And Ehmke went out and fanned thirteen men for a new World Series record. Mr. Mack had his two aces, Grove and George Earnshaw, ready to go in the second and third games, and one contest in the win column without using them. Most managers are hunch players, and in playing hunches Mr. Mack had no superior.

In that Yankee game I felt I might overcome a possible victory by Gomez with a win by Rowe. But I was also playing Crowder for a hunch victory. He'd come to us a few weeks before. He had not been in shape, and we had put him into condition. The change of scenery had done him good, too. Besides, it was his turn to pitch. I felt that if we could beat the Yankees and Gomez with Crowder, Rowe would rise to heights in the second game with a clinching performance.

Through the first four innings my tactical plans looked pretty bad in spots. The only thing that looked good was the "out," the thought which had told me that Rowe would overcome a Gomez victory in the nightcap. Crowder was hammered for five runs and Lefty was sailing along on the fat lead.

Suddenly, as if by magic, the Tiger bats came to life and blasted Lefty out of the ball game with a five-run splurge which tied the score, and then got six more in the next inning to win the ball game. The Schoolboy, incidentally, wrenched his ankle in an early inning of the second game and was in pain throughout the remainder of the game, but he finished and shut out the Yanks. We went on to win the pennant.

It was duly recorded the next day that the

BASEBALL

Tigers had, in that big rally, become first-ball hitters, setting upon Señor Gomez before Joe McCarthy could get another pitcher warmed up; that we stole Gomez's thunder.

The truth is that first-ball hitting is about all you can do with a pitcher of the sort Lefty was that day. When a pitcher is going like that he's hitting dust down the middle of the plate. He will burn in two strikes as fast as he can, and then he has the right, privilege and desire to fool around, even with the most dangerous hitter in the league.

In such a spot you can't wait out a pitcher. Here you lay right into his first good pitch, for if you can't hit that one you stand little chance of getting hold of one when he gets you in the hole.

In such a situation even the greatest hitter in baseball will give the pitcher the same right back at him. If a good control pitcher is burning in two strikes on you before you can get your bat around on the ball, the only way to stop him is to swing on that first one, and keep swinging.

BATTING!

ALWAYS GET OUT IN FRONT OF THE PITCH!

Try never to lose sight of the ball.

KEEP SWINGING!

Somewhere even the greatest pitcher will show a vulnerable sign, for none has been invincible. Even great pitchers get beaten when they are really hot—the hitters just get hotter, and there's nothing that you can do about that. You can call a fireman, but sometimes even he can't put out the flaming rally.

VI

HIT-AND-RUN—THE BUNT—SIGNS

Get that big inning. The big inning is the thing!

There's been a deal of comment about the two great Yankee teams, the '27 versus the '38 edition, and all conclusions arrive at the answer that the greater of these was the greatest baseball team ever put together. I played on a pretty fair country ball club which might not have to hide its face in shame if compared with either of the great Yankee teams.

That team, the 1929 Philadelphia Athletics, was the greatest baseball team with which I ever played, and if it wasn't the greatest in history it wasn't far behind. It had pitching and hitting!

Controversies to the contrary, there is one

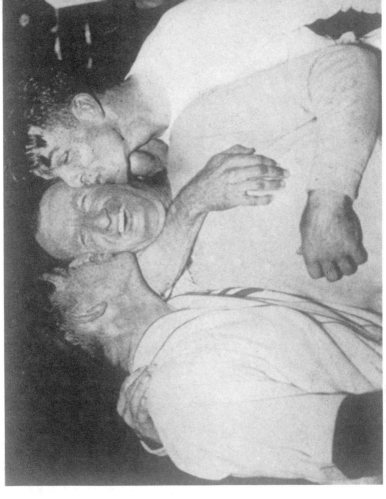

A couple of guys who delivered in the clutch for the author. Goose Goslin flanked by Cochrane (left) and Bridges (right). Goose smacked the hit which won a World Series and Tommy delivered best pinch pitching Cochrane ever saw.

Connie Mack, daddy of all the managers and one of the best.

*A pretty fair manager too, Joe McCarthy, of the powerful
New York Yankees.*

Note DiMaggio's stance as he stands solidly at plate, arching his swing for a crack at ball stopped in flight by high-speed camera.

Photo by Sam André, Pic Magazine

Another high-speed shot, revealing Gehrig's batting form.

Once a familiar American League figure, Babe Ruth scoring ahead of Gehrig after a homer.

Later it was DiMaggio who scored on his own circuit blows.

*Charley Gehringer going up after a wild peg. The Detroit
second sacker one of the game's greatest defense stars and
a fine hitter.*

point on which all experts are agreed, and that is that both Yankee teams and that great combination of A's played for that Big Inning! Those A's mowed 'em down. It was that team which exploded the most spectacular rally in baseball history, an inning that will be talked about for many years to come.

Howard Ehmke had sneaked over that victory in the opener of the '29 World Series, and Grove had made it two up on the Cubs, and then Guy Bush turned us back in the third game. The fourth game found us miserably behind, 8-0, and Charley Root pitching shutout ball. In six innings we'd touched him for exactly two hits.

Simmons greeted Root in the seventh with a home run. Foxx singled, Bing Miller threw up the hit-and-run sign and singled, and men were on first and third. Jimmie Dykes singled, a run scored, Miller went to third, and Joey Boley got a one-baser. Three runs were in, and men were still on first and third. A pinch hitter popped out, but the old hit-and-run came out again, and Max Bishop singled, and the panic was really on. We were now in the ball game, only four runs behind, with men on first and third still.

Then came the break. Hack Wilson lost a fly in the sun, and two runs scored, the hitter, George Haas, going to second. I drew a walk. Simmons, up for the second time, drove a base hit to center, scoring Haas, and Foxx drove me in with the tying run on his second base hit of the inning. Pat Malone, then pitching, hit Miller with a pitched ball, filling the bases, and Dykes rammed a double down the left field foul line scoring two runs; and there the score stood, 10-8, until the end of the game.

It was the big inning to end all big innings!

The fine lead the Cubs had built up in six innings of tight defensive baseball had been blasted into nothing on the wings of one huge rally. One batting spree and the ball game was over—and so was the Series for the Cubs. We took the fourth game the next day.

The hit-and-run weapon played a very important role in that rally, as it does in all big innings.

HIT-AND-RUN—THE BUNT—SIGNS

The hit-and-run combination that is good will hold up a team which lacks sluggers, it will manufacture runs where there were none before, and very often it will break up a really well-pitched ball game.

With men on base, the side in the field is always on the watch for the hit-and-run sign. It's a sign of danger, like a red flag over a dynamite dump. Handle with care or it will blow you to bits. For that reason, a good spy, a fellow with experience in baseball espionage to pick off signs, is a valuable person in the field or on the bench. It takes a very fast double-play combination to stop a good hit-and-run combination. So if you know that the heat is on, you can get ready for it.

Signals, signs of all sorts, have their place in baseball offense. Watching for signs is not a practice that is confined to the combatants. There is no reason why a fan can't steal signs and enhance his enjoyment of the game of baseball. It's great fun and gives you a thrill when you actually know what is coming. That hit-

and-run sign, incidentally, is almost a sure-fire means of pulling a player out of position.

If a hitter can't pull a ball, there is no tonic equal to making a hit-and-run hitter of him. Marvin Owen, with the champion Tiger teams of my day, was just such a hitter. Owen for the life of him couldn't pull a ball to left field. After he mastered the hit-and-run, down in seventh place in the batting order he'd knock in one hundred runs, and put nearly as many in scoring position.

The strength of the hit-and-run is being able to conceal the fact that you are going to put it on. Again it was Cobb who could befuddle the opposition with his sign and deliver the hit. Cobb almost always used the odd rub system. He'd rub himself a dozen times after stepping into the box, and it was up to the base runner to keep track of whether it was an odd or even number of times.

Every time it was odd the hit-and-run was on and then he'd touch himself again and it would be off. He would believe somebody had swiped the sign. Then when the opposition would think they had him doped out correctly, he'd flash the sign again, blast away at a pitch and expect the runner to be off with it.

True enough, with Cobb at the bat, a base runner spent a lot of time diving back into first base, but he would frequently find himself being chased around to third base in the wake of many base hits to right field.

Tris Speaker had a strange sign for throwing up the hit-and-run order. He always chewed gum, and he would never move his jaws as he stepped into the box. When we saw his jaws move or his teeth show, we knew he had on the hit-and-run. One pitch-out and a runner throw-out, and Tris would change the sign to something else.

In a bunt or hit-and-run situation, the sign spy—and the spectator, too—can watch the third-base coach and the hitter. When a sign goes up it will be relayed from the third-base coach to the hitter.

There are many, many signs and countless ways of giving them, and countless ways of passing on the information once you have it.

BASEBALL

You can never tell when a sign will help, or when it'll hurt. Remember that game we spoke of, where Eddie Collins stole all the signs and yet we couldn't beat the Cubs?

A pitcher is up against that sort of thing every time a runner gets on base. As soon as the A's got around to second they'd begin to wig-wag the stolen signals in to the bench for Mr. Mack or to the hitter if he wanted them. Simmons and Foxx never took them. They figured that knowledge beforehand relaxed them too much and lessened their effectiveness.

The code the A's used and the one most generally used when they have the information on the pitch coming up is hands down by the sides for a fast ball, hands curved for a hook, and hands on the hips when the runner has failed to pick up the sign.

A catcher, of course, can mix up the signs so that the wiseacre out there at second base will be crossed up. If he signs in a fast ball and the pitcher serves a hook and the hitter bites —well, things are in the battery's favor. That's one reason great hitters do not take information.

When you've picked off a sign or two, the thrill will come and you'll practise it. Perhaps you'll become as clever at it as Artie Fletcher, for years Yankee third-base coach and topflight sign thief. Arthur is a bandit always ready to confuse the opposition with his own signs, meanwhile stealing the eyes out of your head if you make a move.

The hit-and-run is most effectively snared on the three-and-one or the two-and-nothing pitch. If a team is behind and has a man on first base, that is a perfect time to put on the hit-and-run. The pitcher is almost in a jam, and he must bear down and come through with something right in the vicinity of the plate.

The danger in the hit-and-run comes from having the sign picked off and the catcher call for a pitch-out which traps a base runner off first for a put-out, thus eliminating the jam, the hit-and-run, and trouble, all in one fell swoop. So conceal that sign or you'll get your rally into trouble. And be certain, Mr. Catcher, to call for that pitch-out, even on the two-and-nothing pitch, if you suspect that the hit-and-run is on. The percentage is obvious if you succeed in picking off the runner.

Here the cleverness of the catcher enters the picture. He must never reveal his intention of leaping from the box until the pitch is delivered from the hurler's hand. If he jumps out too quickly, the runner will have time to regain first base. That extra second the catcher must wait is filled with alarming possibilities, but he has to take it to make the pick-off successful.

In trying to lift the signs, watch the movement of each batter. Observe his natural motions, the little things all hitters do when they go to bat. Failure to do one of them, exaggeration of another, may be a sign for the hit-and-run or bunt.

The coaches on the base lines may or may not straddle the coaching box line. Straddling may mean a signal for something. Failure to do it may be another thing. Watch him intently when the situation calls for a bunt, a hit, or a "take" sign. If the hit-and-run is worked, see if he makes any of the motions he made when a similar situation comes up again.

This sort of sign-stealing is of far greater importance than the ability to lift a sign from a catcher of what pitch is coming up.

There are various methods of putting up the sign. One hitter will use an odd count, another a skin-to-skin method, still another cloth-to-cloth, another the peak of the cap business. The odd count was Cobb's pet, others used the second, in which the hitter runs a hand on his face, skin to skin. The cloth-to-cloth is a tricky one sometimes, particularly on a hot day. With perspiration running off his face a batter will step out of the box, take off his cap, wipe the sweat away, and then, incidentally, shake his cap against his pants. The cloth-to-cloth signal has been given in a most casual manner.

The rubbing of the bat is another method. Some batters step out of the box and rub their hands along the bat in certain ways, over the tip, up and down the grip, etc. These are the things I mean by natural motions. Natural movements are what make signs effective, difficult to detect, and hard to follow from one switch of meaning to another.

The American League attack system has, like its defense, been slaughtered by partisan fans in recent years because such fine leaders as Mack and McCarthy do not appear to have much knowledge of the sacrifice. A sacrifice for the sake of putting a lone run in scoring position is really not much of a play in that league —until the last two innings.

For it still goes that one run may beat you a lot of times in the American League, but it will not win as many games for you as it will lose. By that I mean, the number of times a team gets licked by one run, you'll generally find the tying or winning run scored in a big inning —or at least the winning side will approach the tying situation with a big inning.

The bunt has its place in the attack, however. There is no slackening of the importance it plays, and every baseball man sharpens his eyes when he sees a good bunter go up to bat.

The only reason it is used less frequently in

the American League than it was once is the great respect of all teams in the league for the Big Inning.

The two types of bunts are the straight sacrifice bunt, in which the batter gives himself up, and the drag bunt, a surprise tactic by which the batter hopes to gain a base hit.

Different types of players use different stances for the sacrifice bunt. The most essential thing is, of course, to decide on a stance that best suits you, and use it. Personally, I found the most effective stance to be a square one facing the pitcher with the bat held out in front of me on a horizontal plane. Mack batted me second in the A's line-up for several years where a man must be a hit-and-run batter or a good bunter.

The bat should be gripped loosely, and the batter should make his mind up in advance as to the direction in which he intends to lay down the bunt.

One of the dangers of sacrifice bunting is the charging in of the third or first baseman, who scoops up the bunt, whips a good throw to second, thus nullifying the sacrifice and starting a double play. Many sacrifice bunters are clever at bunting hard at the charging infielder, or switching the stance and rapping a hard ball at the man.

Even if the attempt to bunt or hit fails, the maneuver will stop the fielder from charging the batter, giving the bunter more space in which to try the sacrifice.

The drag bunt is most effective against pitchers who have lead in their feet getting over to cover first base, and the fear of it is always a worry to a catcher. Left-handed hitters use it to better advantage than hitters from that other side of the plate. The play is actually under way when the ball is bunted, and usually with the third or first baseman playing deep in his position. The left-handed hitter can work it better by placing the bunt between the first baseman and the pitcher.

To drag a bunt down the first base line, a left-hander holds the bat in a firm grip and without breaking the wrists swings slowly, using the body as a pivot, and breaking into the first stride down the line as the turn is made. Fast men are especially dangerous with this type of bunt.

The bunt-and-run, another use of the surprise bunt, has virtually replaced the squeeze play. Nowadays the bunt-and-run is sometimes confused with the squeeze. In the squeeze the runner commits himself with the pitch, tearing in for home plate with the throw, depending upon the batter to bunt the ball. The pitcher continues his delivery and throws in a pitch-out, giving the catcher a good chance to make a play for the put-out.

On the bunt-and-run the runner at third takes a long lead but does not make a break for home until the ball is actually hit.

The bunt-and-run with men on first and third and one out is a very effective weapon against a double play. Pennants have been won with it. In executing it the hitter aims to push the ball beyond the pitcher, permitting the runner from third to score and the man on first to reach second.

When Washington won the pennant in 1925

it was very difficult to complete a double play against them. In Sam Rice, Joe Judge, Ossie Bluege, Stanley Harris, McNeely and Peckinpaugh the Senators had some very fast men, and adding the speed to a collection of better-than-average bunters they thwarted many twin killings by dumping a bunt-and-run play in with men on first and third. The clever use of the play made Harris' team the toughest team in the league to complete a double play against.

This use of the bunt-and-run shows the efficiency of bunting in unexpected places. Breaks and unexpected developments are always turning the tide of ball games. If you can make a few of the breaks occur in your favor you'll overcome a lot of misfortune when the luck goes against you. This is making the unusual happen when you can, crossing up the hitter with an unexpected pitch, the pitch-out to break up a hit-and-run, and many others. The unexpected employment of the bunt is one of the best uses of it, and one of the things which will keep an infield on its toes.

HIT-AND-RUN—THE BUNT—SIGNS

Whenever the name of Babe Ruth is mentioned, immediately home runs come to mind. But the Babe was an effective and good bunter, when the occasion called for it.

The Athletics knew it. We were playing the Yankees in New York, and the Babe had been on a hitting spree which threatened to knock the boards out of half the outfield fences of the league. We went into the last half of the ninth with the score tied when the New York club got a man around to third base with two out. The Babe came to bat.

Our defense shifted around to the right as we always did for him, with Dykes playing almost over in the shortstop's normal position. Babe dropped a hard bunt down the third base line. The man scored standing up, and while the Babe was no gazelle getting down to first at any time, he'd caught us flat-footed and was safe by half a city block. The ball game was over with a Yankee victory.

This is the sort of surprise play that makes great ball players and great teams.

As fast as a play comes up the smart player

and manager is the fellow who has an answer ready for it. One play of the attack which will not come up more than once in a season occurred in a game with the Red Sox. The Sox had men on first and third and Cronin at bat. Joe fouled high back of the catcher. It was a deep foul and Manager Cronin ordered the first base runner to get ready.

The first baseman tore in to cover the plate. The pitcher remained on the mound. The runner on third base made ready and tore for home as the catcher made the play for the runner going from first to second. The pitcher cut off the throw and heaved to the plate, cutting the runner down cold.

That play had been practised repeatedly. The players involved had become tired of rehearsing it at times. But they were high and happy when it worked and the Sox rally was nipped in the bud.

Meeting the unexpected is half the thrill of baseball!

VII

HANDLING PITCHERS

To me the greatest thrills in baseball, over the long haul, came right behind the plate; diving into runners headed for home, catching the smoky fireball of Lefty Grove in his prime, and handling the jug handle hook of Tommy Bridges.

Handling pitchers is the source of the greatest thrills for a manager, too. Sure, you get a great kick out of having an obvious piece of percentage baseball come out right for you and have the experts term it a piece of masterminding, but when all the chips are paid off the biggest thrill in managing a ball club is in having the right pitcher ready at the right time.

To do this requires an exhaustive study of the hitters of the league—and nowadays if you happen to be a championship manager, of the other league, too. A few years ago, by virtue of having managed the championship Tigers the year before, I was selected to lead the American League All Stars. The stars were gathered at Cleveland for the big game, and we were going over the hitters of the National League.

We came to Arky Vaughan, who was then knocking the hide off the ball at some fantastic average such as .400. Nobody seemed to know much about him, though something had been offered about all the previous hitters mentioned. Finally I asked if there wasn't somebody who knew something about him.

"I don't know how we can be expected to know his weakness," piped Lefty Gomez, the starting pitcher for our side; "those National League teams are playing against him all the time, and nobody over there seems able to get the guy out."

Too often pitchers forget to get in shape. Many of them do not know that legs are almost as important in their trade as arms. Paradoxical as that statement may sound, it is the truth. You've got to have good strong legs able to go the full route.

A pitcher's legs often stop him before his arms. You notice, as the legs get tired and the pitcher loses his stuff, that he gets tired just standing around out there on the hill. And when that sign appears he will soon be puffing, and that's the time to get him out before he gets wild and loses a ball game beyond recall.

Once a pitcher loses his control he seldom regains it for that ball game, so you are better off with him on the bench than out there walking an army around the bases.

Few baseball fans remember, nowadays, that Lefty Grove was once something more than the control pitcher he turned out to be with Boston. Lefty suffered from a fault, common among good strong pitchers with little experience. He took his eyes off the plate during his windup—an error that frequently happens when young pitchers are concentrating on their windup.

The windup is important. Fellows like Marberry, Bob Feller and Bridges attribute some of their effectiveness to the windup. Feller cocked his foot high in front of him; so did Dizzy Dean. Earle Whitehill used to make a full pivot, and Ted Lyons had a herky-jerky motion that was hard to follow. Rookies sometimes concentrate on the stuff they are putting on the ball and on the skill of hiding the ball from the batter until it is delivered. It is not uncommon to find that even so great a pitcher as was Grove in the beginning of his major-league career, is completely ignoring the most important part of pitching—keeping his eye on the plate.

This fault is more often found with the minor leaguer and the sand-lotter who, I guess, pitches by instinct.

Grove had so much trouble with his control that he was walking too many men in his first season with the A's. We had come up together and, as I just said, it was a thrill to catch his magnificent fast ball, but I never could figure out why he walked so many men. In his first year up he passed well over 100 batsmen.

I knew, of course, he was a fast-paced pitcher

when he was going well, which was most of the time in those days.

Taking his eye off the plate and hurrying his pitches caused extreme wildness with his terrific speed.

One day in spring training Kid Gleason suggested that Lefty try counting ten to himself. In this fashion, said old Kid, Lefty would be able to remember the plate and also slow himself down. It was a perfect corrective for his wildness. His record of base on balls after his first season with the A's is testimony of that.

The doctor's orders were soon grapevined around the league, and all the bench jockeys on the circuit were quickly counting ten on every pitch Lefty made. But it never bothered his control, and they stopped it after a while.

A pitcher like Grove, inclined to wildness, can be helped considerably by the catcher making an easy target for him when it is imperative that he come through with a strike. The catcher crouches low and holds his mitt up right over the plate. The mitt and the low crouch form a good strike target.

BASEBALL

The catcher makes the target at which to shoot by framing the mitt in the square over the strike zone made by the catcher's two knees and the points of his shoulders.

In getting pitchers ready, control, wind, and legs are the items at which a manager must shoot. The stuff a man has is his own lookout. You might help him to gain control by some such method as Kid Gleason taught Grove; or you might tell him how to throw a curve. But beyond telling him these things there's little you can do.

All managers can make mistakes on pitchers. There's the story that Cobb, when he was manager of Detroit, told Carl Hubbell he'd better drop that screwball because no arm could stand the strain.

Many things occur, real or imagined, to take toll of a pitcher's effectiveness. In some of these a manager can help him. In others he's helpless. It is, of course, incumbent upon a manager to watch a pitcher who is heading into a slump. A few one-run losses and even the greatest pitcher will begin to think that he's losing his stuff.

In such cases you will find them fooling with trick deliveries, new curves, change of pace, dipsy-dos and countless other dodges which the so-called "brains" pitchers employ. They recall such cases as that of Wes Ferrell who pitched so effectively for the Red Sox after he was, to all intents and purposes, washed up. From a press-box seat Ferrell had a "nothing ball." And at the plate hitting it, it was just about that. What he had was superb control, an endless file cabinet in his mind of the likes and dislikes of every batter who faced him, and, not to be underestimated, confidence that he could still win.

Lefty Gomez, a few years ago, ran into a streak of bad breaks and fooled around with freak deliveries and wound up the year with more defeats than victories.

Fooling around with your delivery may cost you control, and without control you fall heir to that substitute for base hits for the opposition—the base on balls. When the going is toughest, when the breaks are going against you, is when you must have confidence in your ability to come through in the pinches.

Pinch pitching isn't always reserved for the relief hurler who strides from the bull pen to usurp the hero's role and walk off with the pitching honors after retiring a rampant side in a hot rally. In the clutch, a pitcher needs his confidence and control more than anything in the world.

Perhaps the greatest display of confidence in his ability was that shown by Tommy Bridges in the greatest job of pinch pitching it was ever my privilege to receive. The Tigers were playing the Cubs in the sixth game of the '35 World Series. We'd blown two leads and come from behind to overtake the Cubs, and matters stood at 3-3 as Stanley Hack came to bat in the ninth.

Tommy sent up a hook and Hack blasted it for a triple. It was 100-to-1 he would score. Bill Jurges came up and Tommy broke a tremendous hook that hit the dirt two feet in front of the plate. There was only one thing I could do, get down on my knees and try somehow to block it. Luckily I came up with it.

Tommy went to work. He threw six of the most puzzling, hardest-to-hit of his special "jug-handle" hooks I ever saw—and, in two years until then, I'd caught some fancy curves from Bridges. Jurges went down swinging on about the sixth curve. French put him into a hole with one strike and three balls, and again Tommy went to his hooks and forced the rival pitcher to bounce to the box and was thrown out.

It wasn't until he had two men retired that Tommy tried anything but a hook. Then he threw a fast ball and Augie Galan flied out on it.

Detroit was out of the inning by virtue of the greatest piece of pinch pitching I'd ever seen, certainly that I'd ever caught!

I opened the Detroit half of the inning with a single, and Phil Cavaretta came up with a line-drive smash of Gehringer's down the first base line which looked as if it would go for two bases. And then Goose Goslin went to bat.

BASEBALL

Goose fouled off one over first base and then singled to right center and I scored the winning run of the game and the World Series. That inning gave me the greatest thrill I ever had in baseball.

I'd be less than human if I said that scoring that winning run wasn't the greatest thrill, but as I look back on it the whole inning was one exciting development after another. Bridges' near-wild pitch, and stopping it; his superb confidence unshaken as he fanned Jurges; the retiring of the next two batters, and our side safely out of a traffic jam such as wins the average ball game.

When fans get together and begin to talk baseball thrills, and it comes my turn to answer, they want to know about Grove's fireball, and Rowe's great control. Then, in order, come the great streaks of these pitchers. By a freakish coincidence I caught most of the games which both of them pitched to tie the American League record of consecutive victories.

Streaks put pressure on the pitcher and everybody connected with the club. Rowe's was hard on a young pitcher; Grove was touched by the pressure after about the tenth game.

The contribution of luck to these streaks is usually overlooked in the exciting drama of another victory. But along about the twelfth game in Rowe's streak a thunderstorm held off ten minutes and saved the streak and pressure for him.

Washington had us beaten by two runs in the eighth inning. The thunderstorm looked as if it was ready to open up and drench the ball game and wash Rowe's consecutive streak into the Potomac. In the ninth we got two men on base and Hank Greenberg exploded one of his power punches and drove a ball close to 400 feet over the right-field fence. A home run over that fence is a rare item, but one hit by a dead left-field hitter like Hank was equally strange.

In the last of the ninth it began to rain. Ordinarily, under such circumstances a team might begin to stall, for in the event of rain washing out the game the score would revert to the eighth inning where we were losing by two runs. Now we were ahead a run and the Senators had two men on and two men out. It got so dark you could hardly see the ball. Lights were turned on in the back of the grandstand to avoid injury to the spectators in case there was a rush for shelter.

Rowe really rose to great heights in the spot. He fired three fast balls right down the middle that the batter could not see, fanning him for the last out; and, as we walked off the field, the deluge came.

The pressure of such streaks is fierce on the man. Lefty, when he got more than ten straight wins, had a number of one-run games. The tight ones were making him and all of us nervous, and finally it was a tight one that caught up to him.

He'd won sixteen straight and was going after his seventeenth to break the record for the American League when we went into St. Louis. Dick Coffman, later a successful relief hurler with the champion New York Giants, was nominated to go against Lefty.

HANDLING PITCHERS

Through eight innings both pitchers performed like masters. Each was able to turn back the enemy without a run, Coffman really hurling one of the finest games of his life. In the last of the ninth the Browns got a man around to second base. Another man smashed a line drive to left field and Jim Moore playing in the sun lost the ball. He misjudged it and it went over his head, the run scoring. And there went Grove's streak.

Lefty's streak occurred in 1931, seven seasons after he'd electrified the baseball world. Rowe's came in 1934, his second year on the big wheel and his first as a regular pitcher. He was the mainstay of the Detroit staff, virtually a recruit pitcher.

After that Washington break, Lynwood was due for some hard luck. We went into Philadelphia after that, and the pressure was really on Rowe. Interviews, telegrams, telephone calls, autograph requests came en masse. I doubt if he got three hours' sleep the night before the game.

Shibe Park had not seen a crowd such as

turned out for Rowe's great effort since the A's
and Cardinals had fought in the last game of
the World Series of 1931. The gathering was
announced as 33,000 and I guess there was an
added 1000 or 1500 watching the contest from
the roofs across the street from the rightfield
fence.

The autograph hounds pestered Lynwood
until he went out to warm up for the game. A
couple of feminine admirers even came into
the masculine sanctity of the dugout. The pressure was not alone on Lynwood; it had per-
vaded the entire club.

Our exhibition in the opening game of the
twin bill was not one to inspire an expert. We
were beaten by sound hitting of the A's, but we
also booted a few chances around just to show
that we were well tightened up for the grand
effort.

It was my judgment that the added rest waiting through the first game would give Rowe
time to settle down and get him into better
shape to make the effort. I felt, however, that
it wasn't in the cards for him to win.

HANDLING PITCHERS

In our turn at bat in the first inning, we got two runs. Rowe had won many games in that string by such a margin. On that very trip he had beaten the Yankees by such a margin, after twisting his ankle in an early inning. And then, as now, when you still the Yankee bats you're doing something.

But almost from the first pitch of the game I knew he didn't have his stuff. Goose Goslin made a catch in that first inning which was nothing short of highway robbery. But the A's got to Rowe anyway. However, Lynwood was always a slow starter, and in the second inning it looked as if he might come on, and I thought perhaps we might get some of those runs back and help him break the record. But by the sixth it was all over. He was out there with nothing, so I withdrew him.

I can honestly say I was glad the streak was over. I wished that Schoolboy had broken the record, but since he did not I was happy that he'd been beaten and relieved of the pressure. He pitched better ball for the remainder of the season, when we won the pennant. The jitters lifted from the other men and we played better baseball afterward.

There must be something about that sixteen straight, now held by Walter Johnson, Joe Bush, Lefty, Lynwood and Johnny Allen. Allen had rolled up sixteen straight games and was going after his seventeenth on the last day of the season against the Tigers when Jake Wade set the Indians down with a shut-out. Will anybody ever get over that sixteen? That's hard to say. Records were made to be broken.

A look at Hank Greenberg's or Jimmie Foxx's home-run production is another example of pressure bothering a ball player. If the newspaper boys had not commenced to run Hank's and Jimmie's homers beside the record of Babe Ruth in thermometer fashion, either of them might have tied or even broken the record.

The pressure gets the best of them.

Another thing about streaks is that managers get conscious of the pressure of public opinion. It was not true with Rowe because he beat everybody in the league. He set down every club in the league at least twice except the Athletics. He knocked the Philadelphia club over in the early stages of the string and was defeated by them in the second start against them.

But if a manager were to skip a start for a pitcher in a streak, the public would accuse him of picking his spots. I recall that, when I was a youngster, managers were often accused of picking spots for their stars. Sometimes they do, and with legitimate reason.

Temperament is a consideration in relief hurlers. Some pitchers can do anything. Others cannot start a game. Still others cannot relieve. You'll find some who detest batting practice to the point where they make a nuisance of themselves avoiding it.

Batting-practice pitching is becoming something like a lost art, with many clubs retaining the same pitcher on the rubber for the practice sessions day after day. Managers, coaches, and utility men will sometimes perform the task.

The essential thing in a batting-practice pitcher is his ability to get the ball over the plate with good control and an average amount of speed.

If you have a well-manned staff and the batting practice is pitched by some regular persons assigned to that task, you may find one or two men not getting enough work. It is a good policy to pitch a regular moundsman in a relief job in such spots.

A couple of years ago Carl Hubbell pitched in relief roles a great deal. Terry said Hubbell did not like to pitch batting practice and chose the relief roles himself rather than perform at the hitting practice.

Frequently star pitchers cannot be used as finishers. They are temperamentally unsuited. I cannot remember ever seeing Charley Ruffing in a relief role, and Lefty Gomez never was impressive as a finisher.

It is common for star pitchers with a first-place club to have trouble with second-division teams. Just as I have never believed in the efficiency of starting an ace against an ace, I have never believed in throwing a good pitcher against a club he has trouble beating.

HANDLING PITCHERS

Handling of the pitching staff is one of the most important jobs of a manager.

The four best men on the staff must be selected for the starting staff, and there must be two men who are good at relief roles. In the relief roles, as we have pointed out before, you must have men able to step into the clutch and come through with their best stuff. They must have control, a fast ball they can fire through at top step for an inning or two, a sinker which bites into the dirt and makes for double-play balls, or a curve that is hard to get to in quick fashion. The men cited heretofore were perfect examples of good relief men—Marberry with that fireball in the dark shadows of a late afternoon, Wilcy Moore with his funny sinker ball, and Johnny Murphy with his tricky hook.

Gomez explained that he was better if he could work himself into a starting assignment over a twenty-four-hour period. There are other men, of course, who can take the call right in the midst of a rally and walk out from the bench and stop it.

Handling each pitcher in his proper order is

a matter of individual discovery. Just as a catcher must learn how to get the best out of each pitcher he is asked to receive, the manager must learn by the process of elimination how best each individual pitcher will work.

In the major-league club staff of at least eight or nine pitchers, it is essential to give it enough work so that it is effective. Things are always cropping up which will interrupt the order of your starting pitchers—injuries, ineffectiveness against certain clubs, and insufficient rest when the entire group seems to collapse and it takes all of the staff to win, or lose, a ball game.

In a championship race, the odd games present a relief, a burden, and a help all at the same time. Using your best pitchers against the topflight teams, you can generally depend upon the "fifth, sixth, and seventh" pitchers to win a certain number of the games with the second-division clubs.

There's a double reason for this. On a staff there will always be a man who is not a starting pitcher, who will be able to beat second-division clubs. Not simply because they are second-division clubs, but perhaps because the odd man who is not a regular starter—maybe a fellow who requires lots of rest between starts—will be effective to handle certain clubs.

When the A's were burning up the baseball world a few years ago, Grove was their best pitcher. Washington was much of the time less than a ball of fire. Yet the Senators with a left-handed batting order, supposedly weak against left-handed pitching, gave Grove more trouble than any team in the league.

Charley Ruffing was another example of this. He was very effective against the Clevelands, but it seemed impossible for him to get by the Browns, habitually a last-place club.

It may be that the good pitcher is primed for a meeting with the star aggregation and unable to work himself to an effective pitch against lesser opposition. Whatever the reason, it is true that the second-division teams very often give the better pitchers more trouble than the topflight teams.

So you have the policy of using the odd men against the teams sunk deep in the second division; and saving your best men for the teams in your own back yard. Naturally, this is not a routine that is followed too closely. Because, when the heat is on in a close race, the championship club is the team which holds its own with the topflight teams and annihilates the lesser clubs. Remember, there was a year in which the Yankees defeated the last-place club twenty-one out of a possible twenty-two times.

Picking the spots, so-called, is nothing more than playing the percentage. If a pitcher has trouble beating a club, why pitch him against it consistently? If you have a man on the team who is effective against that particular team, that is the man who should get the assignment.

Of course, in World Series the ace-versus-ace theory, the spot pitchers, everything goes into the discard. In a short series where every move is important, you come out with your best on every play. Play your aces as long as they hold out.

If your ace gets beaten, come back with him as soon as he can go, perhaps in the third game, as we did with Rowe in a relief role in the '35 series; Dean and Dean against us for the Cards in '34.

In the short series it is always the aces that take the tricks.

VIII

STRATEGY AND PSYCHOLOGY

THE percentage is always with you in the long run, if you play it.

There are no unmistakable signs that a pitcher has lost his stuff and should be home eating his supper instead of pitching, or that your batting power is going to collapse completely and finally. But there are certain warnings for which you can watch.

Strategically, the bull pen is the most overlooked and underestimated position. Its importance cannot be overemphasized. There a young ball player can pick up a lot of knowledge about the game of baseball; and the more a man plays major-league baseball, the more he must learn about it. And that does not mean for the big leagues alone. Even in sandlot or col-

Never, if it can be avoided, give a base runner room to slide around you.

Always have possession of the ball before you put it on a runner.

Making the runner come to you doesn't always pay. Sometimes a bad throw spoils the plan.

Try always to guard that plate with some part of your body.

lege baseball, in the industrial or Class D circuits, the pitcher waiting his turn to relieve a mate can pick up a lot of baseball.

Up in the big top, battling for position with contending teams in a championship race, the bull-pen catcher, manager, tactician, or whatever you want to call him, is a very important link in the chain that makes up the composite —champion!

Having the right pitcher ready at the right time is one of the big tricks of baseball. Alert managers would always be ready with the best pitcher if they could anticipate a collapse, but they cannot.

One of the most common grand-stand manager's beefs is that the manager does not remove a collapsing pitcher soon enough. "He left him in for one more hitter," or "One-more-hitter Ethelbert we ought to call that lame-brain," they'll squawk.

If these oracles would only look into the bull pen they would discover that "one more hitter, and still one more," is better against a chap who has been working and is losing his grip on the game than to bring on a cold-armed hurler and send him to the chopping block to get his brains knocked out. Substituting a pitcher who is not warmed up and ready is worse, much worse, than giving the waning hurler a chance to pull out of his own slump.

There are exceptions, of course. Oftentimes in major-league circles you will see a pitcher walk from the dugout to the mound and pitch a side out of a hole. This is a rare type of smart control pitcher who requires very little loosening up; a man who has taken a good workout before the game and remains loose and ready for two hours or so afterward.

A weakening pitcher, however, has a much better chance of staving off disaster than the cold reliever has. If he knows that relief is coming—that there will be only one more hitter, or that the inning in which he is working is the last—the tiring pitcher can sometimes pull himself up by the bootstraps and give that final spurt, like a sprinter heading for the tape. He calls on all his cunning and reserve, and may get out of the jam without further trouble.

STRATEGY AND PSYCHOLOGY

In a situation where a pitcher is getting tired, much depends upon the hurler's knowledge of himself. A catcher who asks a pitcher if he needs help must have some doubts, and next to the pitcher he should know best. He gets to know the speeds of a pitcher's stuff better than the pitcher himself.

Many times in my career I asked pitchers whether they did not think they needed a little help, to get the surprised look of an insulted artist. Once I asked it of Lefty Grove when we were kids breaking in.

"Get back there and do the catching, I'll do the pitching," he snapped.

I went back and he nearly tore my hand off with three fireballs that the hitter still hasn't seen. Lefty had been unconsciously letting up, and when he got sore at me he wanted to knock me out of the park with every pitch.

I used to do that with Earnshaw all the time. He'd get so sore at me that he'd try to knock me down with a fast ball.

Other times you could ask Grove whether he

needed help and he'd admit that he was getting tired. He knew it.

Now, the bull-pen catcher three or four hundred feet from the action must keep his eyes and mind on the pitcher as much as the catcher in the game. He must be a tactician, a teacher and a mind reader, all at the same time.

Situations do crop up similar to that one we cited when the Tigers set upon Gomez and pounded him for five runs before McCarthy could get relief to him.

That frequently happens with control pitchers. The opposition never fools around with men who are cutting down two strikes on you before you get set at the plate. The hitters get ready and are swinging at anything that looks like a strike, from the first pitch of the ball game.

If two men ram that first ball into base hits, or extra base hits, the bull-pen catcher and the game's catcher must, of necessity, run a race against time. The right relief man must be warmed up hurriedly and made ready for delivery to the box.

STRATEGY AND PSYCHOLOGY

The catcher in the game must slow down the pitcher on the hill. Make him work on the next couple of batters by tossing in stuff that is good but not too good; a few waste balls; toying around with the hitters even at the expense of a run. The relief man is in a spot; he must get ready for action quickly. After one hitter, the man may be ready and pitching fast. Then the control pitcher can get back in stride, try to pull out by himself.

But when the jam is on, and a relief man is not ready, the strongest pitcher in the world must stall and take his time until the relieving hurler is ready.

So, that fellow out there in charge of the bull pen is a sort of unsung hero of the championship club. Aside from the sudden rally that blows a ball game higher than a kite, he must be using his knowledge of the pitcher working, the wishes of his manager, the progress of the game, and, incidentally, keep those young fellows sent out to his care interested in the ball game rather than in the plans for the evening.

Knowing when to call on the firemen to

squelch a rally is one of the fine arts of managing a ball club. And having a man to call to put the fire out is a big help, and can make any manager look good. When in doubt in the choice of relief hurlers, always pick your best man.

As we have noted before, Murphy was important in the record-breaking performances of the Yankees in winning three consecutive World Series titles. Fred Marberry helped Detroit to that first American League title between 1909 and 1934. When the shadows lengthened along the infield in the haze of late afternoons, old Firpo would kick that foot into the air and fire through a ball which looked as fast as Walter Johnson's or Grove's in the palmy days of their careers.

That name "Firpo," somebody told me during that first season with Detroit, Marberry did not like. I had not known it. Around the league you begin to call the men on other clubs the names the newspapers give them, unless you happen to know that their teammates have other nicknames for them.

STRATEGY AND PSYCHOLOGY

I naturally had assumed that Marberry's nickname was Firpo, but when I was informed that he did not like the name I changed that.

"If he doesn't like Firpo, Fred is all right with me," I said. "From now on call him Fred; 'cause a guy who can put out a fire like he can must be kept happy."

Relief hurling and pinch hitting have much in common—and as a matter of fact there is a difference between pinch pitching and relief pitching in the lexicon of the manager. A relief hurler who comes on in a clutch and gets a club out of a jam has turned in a job of pinch pitching rather than relief pitching.

The reliever in the strict sense of the word is a hurler who relieves; a pitcher who replaces a pitcher in no particular trouble, or who has lost a game beyond recall.

That, by the way, is a good spot in which to drop a young pitcher inclined to nervousness and a feeling of awe at the fact that he's suddenly found himself in the big show and gets the jitters when he gets out there on the mound.

BASEBALL

We were talking, however, about the pitcher who is coming on with the house about to catch on fire. He must come in the right spot. He must be ready. He must be a pitcher with courage, ready to give everything he's got from the first pitch. There are some men who can come into a ball game and never give the scoreboard a thought; others want to know exactly what the situation of the game is. They have the knack of getting into the game better if the heat is less intense—or more intense—than they had anticipated. They want to stop the jam, and with an extensive knowledge of hitters, their strength and weakness, they want to know just exactly where they stand.

The pinch pitcher must have superb control and confidence, and so must the pinch hitter. Earlier we mentioned the pinch-hitting episode of Frank O'Doul in a World Series game, and that brings to mind the sort of confidence a pinch hitter must have. But here we are concerned with what sort of hitter to use in what situation.

Times out of number a manager will hear

catcalls during the campaign when his team is a run behind, a runner on second, and he decides to use a pinch hitter. The stands demand that some other player be used. The reason for the selection of the particular hitter is usually quite obvious. The first rule is never to use your best pinch hitter until the last ditch has been approached; or when the winning run is on base. You can only use him once, and where and when to use him is always bothersome—to the fans.

Their guesses sometimes are right, but never when they would have the manager whose team is behind use the good pinch hitter to start an inning, replace a pitcher with two out and nobody on, or to move a run around from first. The lesser lights are used in these situations. When the runner gets to second or third, and the last ditch has been approached, then send up that good man.

Oftentimes your best pinch hitter will be a line-drive man. Sure he's a terrific hitter, perhaps, but he does not hit fly balls very often. Well, with an important run on third base and one out, it is not percentage baseball to send him to bat when a fellow with a far smaller batting average may deliver a fly ball!

Winning spirit, I suppose, you'd call the mental attitude of the good, or great, relief pitcher or pinch hitter. He's necessarily impervious to criticism, jockeying by the enemy, or the catcalls of the fans.

Each is at his best, relaxed and confident when the heat is on.

The winning spirit in baseball, golf, or fighting is a quality that is as much of a requirement as power hitters, sound defense, and good pitching. The most perfect mechanical players in the game are unable to amalgamate their assets into a championship array unless there is a leadership, obvious and expressed or unconscious, on the ball club.

Instinctively a manager will turn to one or two players to carry the burden of the winning attack. In Philadelphia, when the A's were riding herd on the American League, I had a great time with Mr. Mack when things would go wrong; if I didn't catch it, Jimmie Dykes carried the burden, and when he let up on us it would be Eddie Collins who got it.

In Detroit, when I had become a manager, the burden of the load would shift with the spirit of the team. Pete Fox was a flaming spirit through stretches, then it would be Billy Rogell, Jojo White, Hank Greenberg, or, as in the case of the World's Championship team, Goose Goslin.

Confidence, I guess, is the one essential to the winning spirit. And in major-league baseball, the diamond star's confidence takes an awful kicking around—as do his private and public life, his likes and dislikes, his pride and prejudice.

There is a practice in baseball called jockeying, a little behind-the-scenes game in which the fans do not participate; it enlivens the contest on the field and gives the stars something to think about.

Usually, the jockeying is directed at star players and aimed to break their concentration. Some fellows, like Cobb and Ruth, were pretty much immune because the opposition didn't want to get them mad. As Mack used to say, "Keep Ruth laughing and happy," and "Above all, don't get Mr. Cobb mad at you. He'll hurt you if he gets mad."

Even your best friends will jockey you!

Mule Haas and Jimmie Dykes were friends of mine of years' standing; we'd played on the same team, and yet these two acid-tongued birds gave me a terrific going over on everything I ever did, or tried to do, as a manager.

That Athletics team of the old days, incidentally, was as ruthless and bitter a collection of jockeys as ever pulled on a spiked shoe. We formed a swashbuckling, arrogant, confident band of fellows—most of us rookies—in 1925, and we thought we were going to ride roughshod over the league. And we were going through the motions of doing just that.

On a western trip we'd got on Cobb in a series in Detroit. Mr. Mack had warned us not to go to work on him, saying, "Leave that fellow Cobb alone, don't get him mad at you." But being young and foolish we thought the old gentleman, who'd been around since the league started, didn't know exactly what he was talking about.

We went into St. Louis for a series with the Browns, and for some reason or other commenced to turn our wrath and tongues on Ken Williams, a slugging outfielder, George Sisler, one of the finest gentlemen who ever played, and Marty McManus. Urban Shocker was pitching against us, and we went along all right in our swashbuckling way until the ninth inning of the first game. Sam Gray had a 3-to-1 lead, there were two out and two on, and Ken Williams at bat.

Gray was so cocky and confident that he selected the two-and-nothing ball as a place to try out a new pitch on which he had been working. Sam said this pitch would "sail" and he sailed it up to Williams who sailed it out of the park.

The Browns beat us 4-3. They beat us the next day, and in the last game of the series. What had been a five-and-a-half-game grasp on first place was fast dissipating when we headed for Detroit. Remember, on our previous trip we rode Cobb, and he had told us in parting that he would knock us out of the pennant on the next trip around.

Well, he went wild. He got twelve hits in sixteen times at bat in a short series. He stole everything but the home plate and would have taken that except the series was being played in Detroit and he owned it anyway. He rode us unmercifully, fielded like a combination of Speaker, Hooper, Ruth and himself. He was in every argument, and in the beginning or payoff spot in every rally; in short, he had quite a time for himself.

Before we left town we were in second place, and before we could get hold of ourselves we lost thirteen straight. The swashbuckling arrogance of a bunch of fighting kids had contributed immensely to the slump which cost us the pennant. Our confidence could not stand up when the pressure got tight. The jockeying had paid dividends—for the opposition.

The most amusing "jockeying" experience I ever had, however, was provided by, of all people, Judge Kenesaw Mountain Landis. It was during the Cubs-Philadelphia series of 1929. We had started the series with a fine appreciation for invective and were hurling it from bench to bench across the infield until the air around the home plate was blue.

Lots of these sounds, none too refined, carried over the dugout aprons and into the ears of spectators in the immediate vicinity of the players' benches. After one of the games, Judge Landis issued an order putting a stop to the language and threatening a sizable fine on any parties guilty of disobedience to the order.

We read the announcement and went to the field. The game was at Wrigley Field, and just before the umpire called the game I walked over in front of the Cubs' bench and yelled:

"Hello, sweethearts, we're going to serve tea this afternoon, come on out and get your share."

Being in Chicago, Judge Landis had ensconced himself in a box adjacent to the home dugout. He never by the slightest movement betrayed that he heard my wisecrack. He did not even lift his chin off the rail.

BASEBALL

After the series, when we had won, the Judge came into the Athletics locker room at Shibe Park and congratulated the winners. He singled out many players individually and paid tribute to them in flattering terms. He never gave me a tumble, sitting over in a corner, glad that the series was over and we'd won. I thought he was sore and was going to pass right over me.

Finally, just as he was leaving, he stopped in front of me.

"Hello, sweetheart," he said; "I came in after my tea; will you pour?"

Strategy and percentage baseball run hand in hand.

You'll always find that the smart and daring pitcher is the fellow who gives his best in the clutch, and gives no thought to experiment. Heretofore, I've mentioned that Schoolboy Rowe had a habit of toying with the smart hitters in troubled spots. It was not meant in criticism, for Rowe was one of the most confident pitchers ever to walk to the hill—when he had his stuff.

It was cited simply to emphasize that the per-

Two former teammates in a tense moment: Cochrane trying to cut Dykes off at the plate.

*One way of gaining posses-
sion of a station
is to upset the
keeper, as Hank
Greenberg
demonstrates.*

Even great infielders like Gehringer can be upset by a charging, slashing runner.

Ty Cobb, the best base stealer of them all, shows a piece of his technique.

centage is always with the fellow who plays by the book when the heat gets hottest.

With two out in the ninth inning, two runs behind, and the umpires ready to call the game because of darkness, Gabby Harnett got a pitch in the pennant-winning series with the Pittsburgh Pirates in '38, five days before the end of the campaign which won the flag. There was one ball that the hard-hitting Chicago catcher-manager could murder, and that was a chest-high fast one toward the outside. He got it laid up there and poked it out of the park. The Cubs, who had not seen first place since June, moved into the leadership and took the National League pennant.

Here was a perfect illustration of the argument for the best pitch in the jam. Watch that two-strikes-and-no-balls pitch more closely than the first thrown to a good hitter; for the average manager will instruct his hitters to swing at anything good in a rally except the three-and-nothing pitch.

Many, too many, ball games are won and lost on one pitch. Players get careless with a waste ball, or a pitch-out. Carelessness can cost a ball game when a good hitter is at bat; for the carelessness can give that good hitter a waste ball which may be made to order for him. He'll slam it, as did Harnett, and, boom!—there goes the old ball game.

Playing the percentage does not always mean doing the obvious thing. A gamble can sometimes mean the percentage.

There's the story they tell of Rogers Hornsby being called out on strikes on a third pitch which was right down the middle, a fast ball which, ordinarily, the Rajah would have murdered.

But this was a jam. The deciding run was waiting on base. One of the most dangerous hitters and smartest batsmen of all time was there with a menacing bat in his hand. If memory serves me, it was in a game between the Cubs and Giants, when Hornsby was with the New York club. Harnett, back of the plate for the Cubs, called for a pitch that should have made the pitcher swoon. But Gabby had transferred to the pitcher that confidence which I have mentioned before, and without batting an eye the pitcher wound up and fired it in. It was a fast ball right down the middle, and the Rajah took it for a called strike.

"That guy," said Harnett, "hadn't had a ball like that to hit at in ten years. I figured he'd be so surprised that he'd never see it. Which is just what happened."

You can fool hitters like Hornsby once in a lifetime, maybe, but do not take that experience as a standard gamble. Pick a psychological place for a gamble and it may work. At that time it might even be construed to be percentage baseball.

In the use of pinch hitters and relief pitchers, it is always the percentage that counts. You have to have the feel of the ball game in order to do the right thing at the right time; and even then it doesn't always turn out right. But down through the years enough managers have been playing the percentage successfully to make the book play the right one.

Strategy, psychology, overconfidence, and the right amount of confidence can get all jumbled up in a series of hard-luck breaks when a ball club is playing the percentage and the breaks are going against it. The Yankees in '35 went through a series of tough breaks when we won the pennant; the McCarthymen being unable to take a sufficient number of one-run-margin ball games.

I knew, when the Yanks were going through that, exactly how Joe McCarthy felt. When I first took over the reins at Detroit I lived through three weeks of such breaks right under the gun.

We had a good club. Ultimately we won the pennant. But at the beginning of the season everything that we did went wrong. We couldn't seem to take a one-run game for love or money. We lost them 1 to 0, 2 to 0, 3 to 2, and usually by blowing up in the clutch. The players were tightening up. The breaks were bearing down on them and on me too.

One Saturday afternoon in Cleveland we lost a very close game that was a heartbreaker. In the clubhouse after the game there was gloom and almost despair. You could read the thoughts of the younger players as if they were written out on a blackboard for everybody to see. They were wondering what exactly did you have to do to win a ball game in this league. I was commencing to wonder too. So I ordered the door of the locker room closed and called a meeting of the club. Then and there I ordered every man on the club to go out that night and do whatever he wanted to do.

"I do not want to see a single man in that hotel before midnight," I said. "I don't care what you do. Only go out and stay out and have a good time; forget this ball game; forget baseball. Relax."

Some of the fellows felt so bad that I had to stand around the lobby of the hotel half the night to drive them away. For the most part, however, a little encouragement went a long way. Those who wanted to maintain rigid training, despite one-run losses and all, were in the minority. But that was all right with me; that was what I wanted.

Every man was on his honor to show up at the ball park the next day and let the devil take the hindmost. It worked, too. We played Cleveland again on Sunday and the effects of the relaxing period were most gratifying. The boys drummed base hits around the outfield and let loose with sparkling plays in the field. Our pitching had been good right along. On that Sunday it was better.

We won the ball game by a handy margin; got into a winning streak, and before anybody could upset us got into a winning stride, the percentage of breaks finally coming our way, and we won the pennant.

IX

A WORD FOR THE FANS

THE pressure from streaks, pennant-race jitters, bad-breaks blues, all rolled into one bundle, is nothing compared to the pressure on players—often the stars and whole teams—when a ball club gets into a World Series.

The fans really get so that they own a ball club when their favorites get into the play-off for the championship. The advice from the field boxes or bleachers is nothing compared to telephone, telegram and mail hints for skin-the-cat with which a field manager is deluged before, during, and after a World Series. "The customers always write" was never more fittingly said.

This is all part of the game. Without fans

baseball would not be the attraction it is. And when a group of fans get an idea that a manager is not giving a ball player the right break they hound the manager, pleading for their favorite. Never considering that the manager might want to win as much as they do, and that if their pet would form a link in the strongest ball club he would be in action.

The morning after the Cubs shut out Rowe in the opening game of the '35 World Series, thereby trumping my ace, I got the following letter from an indignant customer:

Early in the morning

Dear Mike:

The best defense is a good offense.

Why not put Walker in center field and get that batting power in the line-up where it belongs?

Would the story have been different yesterday had Fox led off in the first inning with that hit of his? It sure would have been more inspiring than that strike-out of White's. Then when Hank and Goose got those walks, it sure would have raised your hopes if Walker was coming up to bat, 'cause you must admit that the boy hits 'em when they are needed.

A WORD FOR THE FANS

Certainly the Cub pitchers are not worried about White leading the batting order (they have only to look at his batting average to know that if they pitch to him it is a sure out). Imagine the difference they notice when they start off with Fox leading the batting order. Not a weak spot all the way down the list to the tail end. It certainly can give your opposing pitcher more worry than he has with your present line-up.

In the subject of conversation among Detroit fans some accuse you of being personally "down" on Walker, while White is a sort of "teacher's pet" under your wing. No one but yourself knows the reasons why, so use that good judgment of yours and make the right fair decision about the matter.

While Joe Sullivan is credited with pulling the team out of the early slump last spring, how about Walker? Walker played in every game and was batting like a madman. Certainly he furnished some of the inspiration to his mates with his good hitting. But, alas, the Detroit sports writers (so-called) if they do not like a player, will ride him forever, and woe to him that they start to make the goat.

Even with his shortcoming of "being caught off base," Walker *gets on base,* which is more than some of the other players on the team seem able to do.

What do you think Walker would be hitting if he was batting number 4? Here is a guess that the boy would be doing his stuff and be right there where Hank is, perhaps knocking runs in when they are really needed. Somehow Hank seems to knock in runs just in the games that the Tigers lead by a large margin, but in a close game that could be won by one or two runs, Walker has been the boy to knock him in.

Think it over Mickey, and give the boy a break. What say?

> Best of luck for today!
> A Bunch of Tigers Fans

This group of fans overlooked a couple of rather important items: (1) That there was a difference of $2300 to every player on our club and the loser's share of the purse, and (2) most important, that Lonnie Warneke offered a puzzling sort of resistance with a beautiful four-hit ball game in which only Pete Fox got two hits. White, leading off, and Rowe, the pitcher, got the other pair of knocks.

One of the mysteries of managing a baseball

team is the curious fact that no baseball fan can tolerate a good game by the other team.

It would be as easy to explain that as it would be to explain why Bill Dickey couldn't hit the ground with his bat in the Yankee-Giants of 1936 but tore the place asunder in the series the next year.

The World Series does something to a ball player, just as the big game does it to a boy on the back lots, or as a football player gets it in the big game at college just before the whistle blows.

And just as the big game will make an otherwise ordinary gridder rise to heights, so will the World Series drive mediocre ball players sometimes to tremendous feats, feats they could not reproduce during the regular season for all the money in America.

I guess there will always be one or two fellows around who can play before that big throng and give their best—stars, I mean. Stars of the stripe of Dizzy Dean. Ole Diz was never better than when he was, as he would say, "a-rarin' a-back an' a-lettin' 'er fly." Crowds were tonic to Diz.

In the Yankee-Cubs Series of '38, Ole Diz, who had been in only about five games from July until the series, was asked to repeat a performance he had delivered the week before in helping the Cubs clinch the pennant from the league-leading Pirates. His comeback job on that occasion was magnificent.

And against the Yankees, with only a shade of his oldtime speed and nothing but a lot of cute tricks out there, he managed to stave off the Yankee power for a long time—and he might have won the ball game had not a dinky little grounder rolled between shortstop and third base and into left field with two runs scored on it. Rolled between two ordinarily good infielders!

Of course, with Frank Crosetti and Joe Di-Maggio bolting lightning shots over the left-field wall, even Diz could not find too much fault, but it was a truly great performance of skill and courage he gave until the percentage caught up to him—and the pressure or breaks to Hack and Jurges.

World Series or ordinary ball game, the pressure on a pitcher is pretty tough; but even so, he must never lose sight of the fact that there are others behind him and he must trust them. But when they make a mistake, boot an easy chance, or make an error in execution through a wild throw, or make the play on the wrong man in a jam, the pitcher must be the first one to calm down.

"Those guys make an awful lot of runs for me," one truly great pitcher said to me one day, "so who am I to yell if they want to spot the other birds a few runs. They'll probably get them back."

And one of the freaks of baseball is that the fielder who boots a chance, or makes a costly wild throw, will find himself in a position to win the ball game before it is over. It is another of those percentage things which cannot be explained any more than the fact that the outfielder who makes a circus catch for the last out of the inning, is more times than not the lead-off hitter in the next inning.

The best thing for a pitcher to do who has suffered because of an error is to calm down his mate and do it immediately before the mate begins to believe that every one is sore at him and through sheer nervousness begins to boot away every chance within two feet of him.

The great player will come through to repay a pitcher for overlooking a misplay. He's liable to knock the cover off the ball the next time at bat and drive in twice as many runs as he let in.

Mention of great players brings to mind a common practice nowadays—which is to use left-handed line-ups against a right-handed pitcher and right-handed hitters against a left-handed pitcher. Personally, to me that has always been the bunk. I have always felt if a man could not hit one type of pitching he wouldn't hit another.

And, strange as it may seem, you'll find the great hitters, right- or left-handed, usually are

A WORD FOR THE FANS

fellows who can belt away and keep swinging regardless of the side from which the pitching is coming.

When the experts get down to picking an all-star team they are sometimes prone to remark that Joe Doakes isn't an all-star because he can't hit left-handed pitching. Let's have a look at a couple of all-star teams selected from men I saw in action in my own time, and who stayed around for ten years or more.

First, I'll eliminate the pitchers, because on my teams in action the pitchers are going to be good enough to go the distance and win, but they will also be in there for their hitting power.

If I were to name a staff of hurlers from those I saw who had ten years in action, I'd take Grove, Herb Pennock, Walter Johnson, Waite Hoyt, Ted Lyons, George Uhle, Urban Shocker, Sam Jones and Fred Marberry. That would be a fairly competent staff that would have very little to worry about from Johnny Come-laties trying to push them out of the picture.

BASEBALL

As for a couple of all-time all-star American League aggregations, how about Cobb, Speaker, and Ruth in one outfield, backed by Simmons, Combs and Goslin; with Foxx, Gehringer, Cronin and Dykes in one front line, against Bucky Harris, Lou Gehrig, Joe Sewell and Joe Dugan; and with Steve O'Neill and Muddy Ruel back of the plate to handle the slants of that aforementioned all-star staff.

But we were discussing this penchant for withholding left-handed hitters against left-handed pitching.

What would a manager do facing a left-handed batting order of such an aggregation as this:

Rolfe ....3d B
Gehringer ....2d B
Cobb ....L F
Ruth ....R F
Gehrig ....1st B
Speaker ....C F
Dickey C
Sewell ....S S
Lyons ....P

A WORD FOR THE FANS

Or, to take the other side of the question, a right-handed line-up such as:

```
Dykes ................. 3d B
Cronin ................ S S
Simmons ............. L F
Foxx .................. 1st B
Heilman ............. C F
Meusel (Bob) ......... R F
Lazzeri ............... 2d B
O'Neill .............. C
Uhle or Ruffing ....... P
```

Here's a couple of batting orders to end all tricky batting orders.

But even such an array would hardly satisfy all the customers. You're usually wrong when you lose and only sometimes right when you win.

An anonymous note which always amused me most was the one in which a trade was recalled by the writer. Such as:

Poor Mike:

Why not give Rudy York a chance at third base? You know that he can't handle pitchers. Do you miss Owen and G. Walker?

BASEBALL

Remember, you were in *second* place with them.

There are rumors that your head is not completely healed. Is this correct? Then why don't you go back to the infirmary?

YOU DYKES SUCKER!!!

A Royal Fan

P.S. Give Kennedy his soft pickin's or your name will be mud.

All the fans do not beef, though. Once in a while a card would come like this one: "Mickey: What's the matter with that bunch of P. W. A. pitchers (does not include Bridges or Kennedy)? Are they afraid to sweat or are they just going Roosevelt? Go to it, wake them up. A Fan."

Why an otherwise sane business man, who signs his name as a man in a responsible position and would toss anybody out of his office coming into it with advice, should write such a letter to a baseball manager as the following is really more than I could ever understand.

Dear Mickey:

After considerable study on the subject I have a very good tip for you which I wish you would look into.

178

A WORD FOR THE FANS

By acquiring pitcher Stratton you will make sure of second place this year with the good chance of running first. Stratton, in my opinion, is worth $100,000. Kennedy, Stratton, Bridges would be poison to the opposition.

You should be able to convince the owner that he would make money on the investment. Your gate receipts would be much bigger and at the end of the season your man Stratton would be worth more money than you paid for him.

(Signature)

Then a little extra news for me was added in a postscript in handwriting. The main body of the letter was excellently done on office stationery by a stenographer. The postscript made it personal. It said, "P.S. If he does not make a good showing at Boston tomorrow this is in your favor. Get him by all means."

Another "ordinary fan" wrote at the same time and implored me to get Ostermueller from Boston. ". . . give them Wade & Eisenstat. A fellow in new environment will go places (look at Kennedy & Dixie Walker & Piet) In fact grab any good seasoned performer and to hell with temporary criticisms such as

179

followed the Walker, Owen deal; it's results that count. . . . Methinks that in Kennedy & Hayworth you have two swell pinch hitters; and White ought to be good material for a foxy trade."

But the letter of letters was one imploring me to be a preacher and to model my career on that of Billy Sunday. At the end of five closely written pages the writer came to the point: "Now think about his decision. You have been chastised several times and it seems that God has his eye on you. You get the book *Billy Sunday: The Man and His Message*. Read that book, Mr. Cochrane, even if you don't decide to change your kind of work."

Perhaps you will say that but for such interest there would be no baseball—that if the fans did not earnestly believe they owned their ball club they would have no interest in coming out to watch it play and to live and die with it in victory and defeat. And you are absolutely right. Baseball is the one game in which the fan not only believes he has rights, but expresses his belief.

A WORD FOR THE FANS

There is loyalty bred in baseball as well as the fickleness of the fellow who is always on the winning horse. That loyalty is best expressed by a letter dated July 31, 1938, a week before my connections were severed with Detroit Baseball Club. Written in a boyish scrawl, it ran:

Detroit Mich, July 31—38

Mgr. Gordon Cochran

    Dear sir please pardon for this notice
I just cannot help from Liken you
After all the Lies said about you and the club
Its talked that the boys would not play ball
unless Baker was mgr, and Bucky harris
Built them up for your 4 yrs, of success
and that is a Lie

so I only ask you

For the crumbs that fell from your
Table to gain this years victory so
Prove you are the Best manger, in history

very truly

Benjamin Cheers
600 Alger.

P. S. Bridges Wade Auker & Lauson Should sweep this Yankee series

BASEBALL

Such loyalty furnishes one of the pleasanter memories from a pleasant athletic career. There were thrills, too. There will never be another thrill like that of denting the home plate with my spikes in the run that gave us the pennant in the 1935 World Series!

X

EPILOGUE

IN all my career in baseball, or in any sport for that matter, never had I experienced such excitement as that which turned Detroit into a city gone mad with delight the night we won that World's Championship.

Not since the early days of Cobb, back there long before Detroit was the great city it was in '35, had the Wolverine metropolis had a chance to get really hysterical over baseball.

Through the campaign of '34, when we got into the Series and lost out to the Cardinals in a heartbreaker, there had been growing signs of the madness which might come up if we ever won. It grew and grew in intensity as the Tigers swept through the '35 campaign. And then, when we defeated the Cubs, it took off all at

183

once, as I came home with that winning tally. I do not believe anybody knows for certain today whether Goose Goslin ever touched first base. The hordes of wild fans were on the field before the ball bounced in the outfield, safely.

Players were carried from the field on shoulders of fans like conquering heroes. Men, women, children, dogs and candy butchers vied with radio announcers, newspaper reporters and motion-picture stars to shake the hand that had shaken the world—as far as Detroit was concerned. This hand was that of Goslin or Bridges.

Frail, quiet, reserved and unused to display, Tommy shook more hands and got more back pounding that afternoon than a baby-kissing politician passes out in three lifetimes.

The city was at once a madhouse without doors or bars and all the Mardi Gras tossed into one locality. People who had not spoken to one another for years threw their arms around necks of enemies and kissed and made up. Everybody was every other person's friend. Street cars were stopped on their squeaky flat wheels, unable to move at even a snail's pace for hours through the downtown traffic. Hotel lobbies were harder to cross than the Maginot Line. Everybody was a baseball fan. Everybody was an intimate of all Tigers.

Even the newspapers went daffy. There were interviews with players, umpires, bat boys, wives of players and friends of players who knew this or that man when he was a rookie in Peoria. There will be other World Series, of course, and other hysterical celebrations, but for sheer high glee and generosity I do not believe the '35 triumph of the Detroit Tigers will ever be duplicated.

Presents from everybody, from the chairmen of boards of automobile concerns down to the gatemen, were heaped on favorites. Tons and tons of gifts, expressing the esteem in which all the men were held, poured in from all directions—and kept coming for days. I got everything from homemade cake and cigarette lighters to automobiles.

And what a far cry this cheer and wealth and acclaim was from that period of incubation at

BASEBALL

Dover, Delaware! From busses and uncultivated playing fields, to hero-worship, first-class passage, and diamond tiaras for the missus if you wanted them!

That is the road which baseball travels from bushes to pinnacle.

Today, one hundred years after its so-called invention, baseball is a career which finds college men vying with the boys from the sandlots. The reasons are obvious. There are opportunities in baseball today, as there were ten, twenty, forty years ago. These chances are just as good today as in the Golden Era of sports when I broke into the game.

Disillusioning experiences will come, but they must be surmounted—in baseball as in any other pursuit. Remember that even Babe Ruth, when he started in, wasn't the finished ball player he became after years of experience. It took the Babe a long time to reach that incredible string of home runs. In fact, he'd been in baseball fourteen seasons before he reached his peak.

Keep swinging. That's the answer.

EPILOGUE

Keep your eyes and ears open and your mouth shut.

Make a mental note of everything you see. And never forget anything: the stance of a hitter, the movements of a pitcher, the ball a hitter takes.

Frankie Frisch, over a long period one of the brightest stars of the National League, was telling a story about Carl Hubbell, as great a competitor as he was a pitcher.

Frisch told how he'd once had Hubbell throw him a screwball with the bases "drunk" and none out. Frankie deposited Hubbell's great curve against the Polo Grounds fence for a triple.

"You know," Frankie said, "I hit against Carl for a long time after that knock, but as many times afterward as I hit against him I never again saw a screwball. He threw me everything but the pitch I laid against the fence!"

And that is the story of successful baseball.

Watch everything, and try to avoid making the same mistake twice!

GLOSSARY

Bases drunk: Bases full

Blooper: A cheap hit

Bush, or Joe Bush, or Joe College: A college ball player

Can of corn: A lazy fly ball to outfield with one out and a man on third who can't score after catch

County-fair ball player: A show-off; one who runs around and makes a lot of motions doing nothing

Cunny-thumb pitcher: A slow ball pitcher

George Stallings pitcher: A 3-and-2 pitcher; one who gets behind every batter; a wild hurler

Horsecollar: What a slumper gets in box score under H

Humpback liner, or blooper: A lucky, slow hit that just clears infield

Jockey: To reveal an opponent's private life—but loudly, and sarcastically when possible

Pay ball: A ball easy to hit

Pay station: Home plate

Pop-off or Rebel: An umpire baiter

Spaulding Guide: A player who poses, every move a picture